Souvenir

Books by Kathryn Rhett

Near Breathing (1997)
Souvenir (2014)

As editor
Survival Stories: Memoirs of Crisis (1997)

Souvenir

Kathryn Rhett

Carnegie Mellon University Press
Pittsburgh 2014

Acknowledgments

Thanks to the editors of the magazines where the following essays appeared. They have all been altered from their originally published versions.

"Confinements" appeared as "What I Saw" in *The Tusculum Review*.

"Conception" appeared in *River Teeth: A Journal of Nonfiction Narrative*.

"Sanguine" appeared in the online journal *Prime Number*.

"The Last Word" appeared in *Michigan Quarterly Review* and was listed as a notable essay in *Best American Essays 2009*.

"In Transit" appeared in *Harvard Review* and was listed as Notable Essay in *Best American Essays 2010* and given special mention in the *Pushcart Prize XXXIX*.

"Tourist" appeared in *Marginalia* (print edition).

"The Lonely Wanderer" appeared in *Michigan Quarterly Review* and was given Special Mention for Nonfiction in the *2004 Pushcart Prize XXVIII, Best of the Small Presses*.

"The Big Time-Out" appeared in *Crab Orchard Review*.

"Wayward" appeared in *Harvard Review* and was listed as Notable Essay in *Best American Essays 2012*.

"The Travelers" appeared in *The Massachusetts Review*.

Lyrics quoted in "Crown" are from the song "Svantes lykkelige dag," or "Svante's Happy Day," by Benny Andersen.

Design by: Connie Amoroso

Library of Congress Control Number 2014943675
ISBN 978-0-88748-589-3

10 9 8 7 6 5 4 3 2 1

for Fred, Cade, Jacob & Benjamin

Contents

Confinements

I saw the places of confinement. Those first, though I had been walking for a while, away from my Gettysburg home, which had begun to feel confining. After the sidewalk ended, after the neighbors' houses and then the strangers' houses, the black road shoulder wasn't safe enough at dusk, and I saw how the grass of the nursing home lawn would be safer, and so I walked on that. I saw the large white nursing home mailbox, with green stick-on letters spelling out GREEN ACRES. I saw the Adams County Jail beyond the nursing home, and though I had thought of walking past the jail and across the battlefield to the pre-Civil War cemetery (to see the erasure of names, the tilted stones) and then down the rippling one-lane road that let out at Vicky's Country Kitchen, the tacky place with the HELP WANTED and the ALL U CAN EAT SPAGHETTI signs out (and I must admit a bias against the very name Vicky, a former girlfriend of my uncle Garry's who used to get drunk with him between his third and fourth marriages and come searching for him at our place, waving her straw cowboy hat and whooping at 2:00 a.m. in the driveway); though I had originally thought of that route it now seemed unwise because of the dusk coming on with a gray indistinctness, which I saw when I turned into the nursing home driveway, walking as if I meant to be there, walking directly toward the lights, as it happened, of a parked pickup truck. Which was fine, though parked pickup trucks with their headlights on certainly evoked, for me, hunters and good ol' boys who were not necessarily friendly.

I saw the chainlink fence around the back of the jail, enclosing what might be a garden, chopped-off stalks sticking up dry after the winter. Do they actually grow vegetables there, I wondered, and serve them to the inmates. Within a fence within that fence sat a pickup truck with a rack, the kind for carrying ladders and sheets of glass. I saw that the jail had a lovely two stories high rectangular panel of glass bricks, through which I could see a shimmering light-bulb and metal stair bannister. Our home has just such a panel of glass bricks, only smaller and square, glass bricks being the hallmark gesture of a famous architect, Mies van der Rohe, who used them to bring together privacy with light. There was a certain Mies van der Rohe house in Cambridge, Massachusetts, that I had dutifully stood in front of with the other architecture students, to admire the elements of the structure, though I was the limited sort of student whose mind stopped at the glass bricks (the imprisonment of light, their illusory clarity) rather than comprehending the whole. In a jail the glass bricks might be interpreted as less than a beautiful gesture, though the architect had clearly been a thoughtful person vis-á-vis this one particular wall.

I saw, as I walked up the nursing home driveway, that the nursing home had a view, a vista of battlefield hills, flattish slopes extending for a quarter mile before rising up steeply, the farthest hill crowned with a fire tower from which one could see the perpetually burning memorial flame dedicated to the unity of the post-Civil War nation. How had a modest nursing home come by such a view, and could anyone see it?

A few lamps shone behind windows, dimmed by screens or sheer curtains or venetian blinds, and it did not seem that anyone looked out at the scarves of dusk laying down the rules of disap-pearance. I saw how I wanted a realization and how I might get it, cheaply, imagining a woman stuck in her room observing how lucky I was to stride across a landscape. In the context of the woman surrounded by relics who might limp out to a lawn chair on occa-sion, I was one fortunate person. I thought of the ones in jail who couldn't even look out, except from the small exercise yard on the far side of the building with a view of a car dealership, of their real and true confinement, and of the other confinements that had led them to be in the jail. I saw a mint green bus in the nursing home parking lot, on which dark green letters against the mint spelled out GREEN ACRES; underneath, in script, was painted *The Adams County Home*. If that didn't sound pathetic enough to break your heart. *The* home, as if there were only one place in the county for all the old folks to go, as if it were a natural progression for everyone to end up here with the green color scheme and the view of fields where fifty thousand had died, been wounded or gone missing in the previous century (the most blood-soaked piece of ground in America), as if the place was a lovingly homemade and handcrafted depository full of hand crocheted afghans, and that was okay. Maybe it was, maybe it was. Maybe the wheelchairs were lifted tenderly onto the anachronistic bus, which had no contemporary disability access features.

The pickup truck bumped into gear and cruised past me, the driver nodding in a neighborly way (or was it forbidding, as if he'd been waiting to approve or disapprove) out the open window. It was the first nice evening of spring. I walked straight to the back of the property, where the home had another lovely view, cornfields giving way to battlefield and then forest. I walked down the lane of grass along the trampled straw-colored stalks, and saw an animal—just a tip of eyes and fur—drop down a hole, and I saw how enormous holes occurred every few feet and how nobody seemed to care much about trespassers, unlike our neighbors, who all set traps for the groundhog who dug up under their sheds and ate their streaky-leafed hosta plants, and they took the groundhog out ten miles and it always came back. I saw how groundhogs were having their way with the nursing home property. I saw the wispy end of a long frond ascending a tree (it was nearly Palm Sunday) and saw that a squirrel was carrying an entire cornstalk up for a nest.

I hadn't walked away from my house to go anywhere in quite some time, to go anywhere, that is, without a purpose in mind. I'd had a headache for three days, the kind of headache that makes you wonder if you're dying and too stupid—too out of touch with your body, too much living in your head—to realize it, like patients in the days when doctors told nothing and you could just be answering the telephone and cooking broccoli and collapse on your kitchen floor; the sort of headache that makes you give up sugar, alcohol, television, all the sins, even reading, until you are just staring at the wall thinking that rest is what you need, that the rest cures forced on hysterical women in former eras and now widely regarded as patronizing and cruel, that those rest cures are at this moment widely regarded by you as pretty damn good. I used to walk, even run, away from all the houses and apartments until we moved to this town, though I'd thought of the running as futile because eventually I always returned to the house, as if stretched out and snapped back like a rubber band; I always returned, so what was the point of running away?

In this small town there was even less point in venturing out, because I couldn't be anonymous as in the preceding cities and foreign countries and nomadic stops—I was accustomed, in other words, to being invisible. If I kept up this walking habit, I'd be the woman who walked by the jail in the evenings, like the old guy who rode his bicycle in all weathers, or the disturbed man who patrolled the center of town with his crusty little dog. In this town the women wore lipstick and placed potted mums on their steps and glided about in khaki minivans, and I followed the code as far as I could so as to avoid standing out, for essentially I preferred *seeing* to being seen. Walking behind the nursing home, I approached the new agricultural center, for which a man had scavenged our broken garden bench off the sidewalk on junk pickup day the previous spring. He said he'd weld it together and set it in the demonstration garden and that the kids and I should come visit; a piece of us would be in the garden.

How hopeful that had sounded, the town's junk to be resurrected in a garden, and we had smiled as he'd heaved the bench into his truck. I saw how large and clean the new agricultural center was, its parking lot paved black, its saplings circled with mulch and supported with wires. Though I had no idea about the purpose of the large brick and prefabricated metal buildings, off to the side six long curving rows of overturned earth had been marked off with orange-tagged pickets, the beginnings of the garden. As I approached Old Harrisburg Road, I saw my bank, the Adams County National Bank, and for the first time I saw its façade as the architect must have drawn it rather than from the side as one approached the place by car, a façade which seemed sad and colonial, a one-story bank with just a few small windows, made of brick that had a faintly smoked quality, as if it might have smoldered and gone out years ago, but had been kept going with a minimal expenditure of energy. As I crossed the road and entered the shopping center, my safest route home in terms of traffic, I saw that although the shopping center had acquired a more prosperous air with the addition of the Harrisburg Area Community College and a uniform maroon roof above the storefronts, there were still several boarded-up stores, victims of the flood of 1993.

Which was some time ago, now. The shopping center had not recovered from the flood, which had wiped out the entire inventory of a Rite-Aid drugstore, a Ladybug Fashion Store, and its big sister, Ladybug Plus. Those boarded-up stores are the view from our Adams County home, where for several years we could still make out the fading lavender letters of LADYBUG PLUS. I turned my back to the stores and hiked up the small incline to the elementary school soccer fields, where neighbors were kicking a ball at the nearly invisible goal, the night almost dark except to those who were out in it. "Have you been out running?" the mother called. "Walking," I called back. "Taking a loop?" "Yes, a loop," I said, "it's such a nice evening." I crossed the last street to my home. I sat on the breezeway for a while. It was spring, and I was a free person, and not ready yet to go in.

.

Conception

November 19 is Remembrance Day here in Gettysburg, the day that Lincoln dedicated part of the battlefield as a cemetery for the Civil War dead in 1863. That year in July, the dead lay on the battlefields, on the farmers' fields planted with crops and in the summer-green woods where they had taken positions behind boulders and tree trunks. Some lay covered with dirt, and others just lay bare to the weather. When land for a cemetery was set aside, the townspeople moved the dead to proper graves.

As a citizen of Gettysburg more than a century later, I carry no responsibilities as burdensome as moving thousands of dead bodies for burial. My children and I climb the steep trail of Big Round Top, scaling the hill's crowning boulders and dropping down behind them, pushing leaves off of low plaques to learn which soldiers fought where. We acquaint ourselves with the town's history—I was impressed to hear that the main building on the Gettysburg College campus had been a Civil War hospital. Later I realized that nearly every building standing in 1863 had been, of necessity, a hospital, too. A colleague who commuted here from Maryland once asked, "How can you live in that town? You're living on the most blood-soaked piece of ground in America." But this place doesn't feel blood-soaked. The former hospital buildings are bed & breakfasts, or dormitories, or offices. The battlefields roll out like velvet, their hems bordered with silent cannons and marble monuments. Although there was so much death, to my mind it's safely tucked into the past.

Along the sidewalks in the tourist end of town, the ghostwalk guides would disagree. A woman in a hoopskirt holds up an oil lantern as tourists gather in the fall darkness, shivering in their jackets. Swinging by in the car to pick up my daughter from a football game or dance, I see them heading up the hill in a mob, to summon up the local ghosts. As the Ghosts of Gettysburg website says of the men killed here, "Their presence on earth was silenced forever by death. *Or maybe not . . .*"

I had ghosts of my own.

In town, on November 19, there is a wreath laying ceremony at the cemetery. I prefer to visit on Memorial Day, when the town's children march in a parade to lay garden flowers on the soldiers' graves. That's the sort of charm a small town has—one is expected, of course, to have garden flowers. Thanks to the previous homeowners' planting of perennials, we can usually manage a straggly bunch. And Captain Trickey, who owned our house before the previous owners, had planted climbing roses on the south side of the garage that persist, blooming small scarlet flowers, despite our neglect.

My husband and I didn't attend the wreath laying ceremony in 2002 or hear a recitation of the famous address: "Fourscore and seven years ago our fathers brought forth on this continent a new nation, conceived in liberty . . ." Though the opening words have been heard so often that their literal meaning can glide right by, it is odd to think that in the nineteenth century, Americans did commonly mark time from 1776—thus a plantation mortgage document for former family land that my father and I found in a South Carolina courthouse is dated the "Eighty-third year of the Sovereignty and Independence of the United States of America," or 1859. As a country, we were tethered to a different point of origin, then.

My husband and I, busy with work and children, did not often attend community events, and on this night we stayed home as usual and put our two children to bed. Then we sat outside on the breezeway. As of the next weekend we would be thrust into the extended family arena—Thanksgiving, Hanukkah, and the dedication of a memorial boulder for my husband's sister—and occasionally before these occasions we went a little crazy. Drank too much wine and sat out on the breezeway in plastic Adirondack chairs and smoked a few cigarettes. We used to smoke. We didn't anymore. We used to drink too much almost routinely, playing poker with friends, throwing parties at which every scrap of food in our apartment was eaten, the last slices of bread made into toast at 3:00 a.m. Sitting out there on our breezeway too late, wearing winter coats and indulging in old habits, recalled the old "us," the ones who lived in beat-up apartments and traveled overland to Guatemala and moved every year and didn't know what would happen next. November 19 was the first night like that in a while, when we felt romantic, so I remembered the date. That night, without intending to, we conceived our third child.

The first ghost was my dead sister-in-law. To say "dead sister-in-law" or even "cancer diagnosis" sounds unacceptably final. "Cancer diagnosis" had once seemed the beginning of a story—a story she began to write as a memoir—that included revelation and recovery. Then the narrative shut down, and the conception of it changed. Diagnosis equaled death sentence. During that fall after she died in June 2002, I was numb. There was the kitchen phone I would use to call her, the chair I sat in while we talked, the basket filled with printouts about clinics and medicines. There was the calendar that used to look bright white, the pages significant with tests and visits. That fall the calendar sat dead on the counter, a grayish bureaucratic instrument, telling me what to do.

Her widower asked me whether I had dreamed of her. "I dreamed," Tim said, "that she was in a school for the dead, learning all sorts of spiritual things, and so excited to tell me." Sometimes she appeared to me in my mind, and spoke to me in the old way: "Never undervalue the water vegetables," she had said once, meaning that we should eat cucumbers and iceberg lettuce because they held a lot of water, even though they were not the vibrantly colored superstar vegetables like carrots and spinach. Unimportant sentences like that sounded in my ear and then, alone in my house while the children attended school, I would lapse into a reverie of remembrance.

That fall I felt full of death, which is to say, empty. I felt dead inside, scoured out. Sitting at the kitchen table attempting to work, I would rouse myself from paralysis and almost run out of the house to do errands, or go to my brightly lit campus office full of paperwork and email. At work I performed exactly as required, since that fall I was being evaluated. I clicked down the hallways in heels, clicked my ballpoint pen at meetings, wore red lipstick, and taught classes while colleagues observed me, stalking in front of the blackboard authoritatively, eliciting comments from the most reluctant of students. But when I turned off the office lights and went home, the deadness returned. I was only a perfect shell.

"Little Miss Perfect," our neighbor had sneered at me in childhood. Her children had messy hair, unwiped noses, frayed elastic. I always played the princess in our ad hoc performances. Ballet, my chosen sport, aspired to perfection without visible effort or cost. While the rainbow tutu itches, the satin toe shoes hurt, one must dance as if blissful. The high compliments: *she makes it look easy*, or *grace under pressure*. I wanted those compliments, still want them. That fall I was empty. All I was, was an appearance, an apparition of a self.

We lived "in town," where one is seen and remarked upon, whether raking leaves, buying a candy bar at the convenience store, or taking a walk on Saturday morning. When a new neighbor moved in from "the mountain," a rural area on the slopes of nearby South Mountain, she remarked, "Now that I live in town, I won't be able to hang laundry in my pajamas." When I got pregnant by accident during the mournful November of 2002, one of my first thoughts was how it would look: *How sloppy, how embarrassing. At my age. With two children already, and both of them in school.* My life was fine. Or, rather, it *had* been. The square in the indicator window of the home test was supposed to remain white. On a December night, when a pink plus sign glowed into place, I couldn't believe it.

Conceived in oblivion, conceived of as a mistake.

Both of my children had suffered problems at birth. My daughter aspirated meconium, couldn't breathe, nearly died. My son had a hole in his heart. I had Polaroids of both in neonatal intensive care. They turned out fine, unscathed, healthy, without consequence. We were so lucky. Why would I chance it again?

During the black, early winter evenings, we kept finding things my sister-in-law, Kathryn, had given us. They were souvenirs from her travels in search of healing, to see an acupuncturist in the Canary Islands, or the doctor in Bonn who injected chemicals at tumor sites. We found tiny stoppered flagons of Penhaligon's perfumes from England, a rope of pink pearls and a length of silk printed with butterflies from China, and—from an ashram in mid-state New York, from a healing ceremony—a brown string bracelet I used to wear so as to be sure to think of her every day. Some nights when I took it off and laid it on the bedside table I felt free, as if from a welcome but too-long embrace. I found a red-faced Swiss watch misplaced for years, a counterfeit Prada bag that—when I wasn't enthusiastic enough—she had assured me was the "best class of counterfeit available." Now she was gone. One day we would find the last gift.

Being a reasonable person, only if I had become pregnant on the day of her death would I have allowed myself to say aloud a far-out idea like "transmigration of souls." No, it was six months later, now. Outside, the cropped cornfields had gone brown. We were thousands of miles from her deathplace, in Germany. I didn't feel that my unexpected pregnancy was part of the narrative of my sister-in-law. But then later I couldn't un-connect it. Someone in the family had died. And someone new was going to be born.

The second ghost rose like the full December moon over the woods, appearing suddenly to stare me in the face. It wasn't a person, but a promise from the past.

I had promised myself I wouldn't have an abortion. Again. In the fall of senior year in college I'd become pregnant. The night it happened, my best friend from high school had come to visit, confided that she was in love with me, and tried to kiss me. I fled my one-room apartment, and her, for the most heterosexual site possible: a frat boy's bed. When I saw him on campus later, I felt disgusted with myself. Why couldn't I have talked to my friend instead? When I told her I was pregnant, she came to see me again. The Baltimore sidewalks glinted under an Indian summer sun as we walked for blocks, talking and shouting. She grabbed my arm to stop me. "Abortion is a sin," she said intently. She was Catholic. Her moralism made me furious, with the fury of a child brought up in the Episcopal church who had never quite believed that Jesus rose from his tomb, and whose family quit going because the minister was having an affair. Church was full of promises and lies. And she was full of self-righteousness, throwing sin at me as if her being gay was just fine with the Catholic Church. "You will never have to worry about getting pregnant when you don't want to," I snapped, not shutting her up, but shutting up her argument's power over me. "You will never have to feel this way." I wanted no future of child support payments and custodial visits with the frat boy. Neither did I like the image of myself in a black graduation robe, seven months pregnant.

From time to time I have imagined how old that child would be. I have regretted my unwillingness to face difficulty. Yet almost exactly nineteen years later, another November, I felt cowardly again. Why should I be at the mercy of my fertility, at the mercy of a stupid mistake?

My usual doctor didn't handle obstetrics anymore, so I got the young guy. After a pale nurse whispered to him that I wasn't sure about the baby, he turned his big blue eyes on me. "Then I suggest you visit the Tender Care Pregnancy Center," he said. "Do you know of it?"

Sure, I knew the pink-and-blue painted sign, the dingy-looking place over a lamp shop on the outskirts of town. It looked just like the Emergency Pregnancy Center, or whatever it was I had found in the Yellow Pages and called in a panic in college, the place that sounded benign and showed me a film of fetuses in trash cans. But maybe I was wrong. "What sort of place is that?"

He leaned forward, looked at me earnestly. "They'll talk you out of having an abortion."

I felt cold. No longer a college girl who could be pushed around, who would watch that whole film without bolting as if good manners mattered most, I was an English professor. "Then why would you refer me there, when I'm not sure I want to continue this pregnancy?"

We had a silent face-off. He sighed and turned to the nurse. "Have the receptionist set her up at York to talk to Dr. X. Say she wants to talk about options."

At the checkout desk, a woman placed the call. "We have a forty-year-old, pregnant, wants to discuss options," she said loudly into the phone. Just then a colleague came up behind us to pay her bill. I gave my husband a desperate look. "She's pregnant—not sure about it," the receptionist bellowed.

On the way out, I noticed the volumes of children's Bible stories on waiting room tables. How had I ended up living here? Central Pennsylvania was a backwards place, closing its schools for the first day of hunting season. The summer we moved there, an op-ed in the local paper argued that the schools should reinstate corporal punishment in the form of paddling. Working with the school nurse on a breakfast program, I had heard the angry protests of the school superintendent, who believed that breakfast should be cooked at home by mothers. He seemed to believe that holding firm would erase such circumstances as poverty, night shift factory work, and overly long bus rides, and that mothers would magically serve pancakes thirty minutes before the first bell, their aprons tied in pretty bows.

Years before, in San Francisco, I had worked on a screenplay about abortion in Pennsylvania, about smuggling minors across state lines to circumvent the parental consent law. Pennsylvania had a twenty-four hour rule, whereby after visiting a clinic and deciding to have an abortion, you must wait twenty-four hours before having the procedure, and the closest clinic was an hour's drive. The local schools taught abstinence, not birth control. In recently reported statistics for the county, two girls under age fifteen got pregnant; one ended her pregnancy, and one had a baby. Thirty-seven girls from ages fifteen through seventeen got pregnant, and thirty-three of them had babies. The Gettysburg high school has a daycare center.

It was as if I had moved backward in time.

The doctor had made me feel ashamed. My appointment had been for a pregnancy visit, so I had assumed our conversation about my ambivalence would be just the initial part of a full exam. "He didn't even examine me," I said to my husband. "I said I wasn't sure and then he couldn't even treat me like a human being." Over the next week I became angry. The only obstetrical practice in our town of 8,000 wanted to refer me to anti-abortionists. The local hospital did not perform abortions, and the local branch of Planned Parenthood not only performed no medical procedures in their office but claimed to know nothing about where an abortion might be obtained. They said they had never heard of medical abortion, the RU-486 pill that had made so many news headlines. Doctor X in York was an hour away, and who knew what her attitude would be?

The next day, watching minivans cruise up to the elementary school, I scrutinized the mothers, who appeared more grown-up than I felt, with highlighted hair, gold jewelry sets, and coordinated outfits. Had any of them ever gotten pregnant by accident? Had any of them, I wondered, had an abortion? There were, in a recent year in the county, 346 reported pregnancies in women aged thirty and over. Six of those pregnancies were aborted. For a county of 86,000 people, that's not a lot of abortions. Those mothers in their minivans steered expertly, wore red sweaters to the Christmas bake sale. They didn't look as if they made mistakes.

Over the next month I made appointments for abortions and then canceled them, became suffused with happiness when it seemed I was miscarrying at two months, watched numbly the ultrasound movie of a pulsing lima bean, and became resigned to the fact that if I broke my promise I would not forgive myself. I could have my happy planned family, and now that the children were in school, my easier life, my time to write, my summer vacation without chasing a toddler around the pool. But to break a promise like that augured secret corrosion, an interior crumbling with the knowledge that no promise need be kept.

In Baltimore nineteen years before, the medical team had assembled in a white room. They had dispensed Tylenol for pain. A nurse flicked her eyes up at me, her eyes dark brown above a white surgical mask. Surgical masks give the eyes a look of alarm, of seriousness. All of the eyes fixed on me. The nurse held my hand while they revved up a machine. The machine stood like an upright vacuum next to the table. I lay on an exam table as if for a pelvic exam but for the presence of the masked team and the sound, a vacuum with a loud underwhine. I clutched the nurse's hand hard. "One minute," she said kindly, matter-of-factly, telling me how long the pain would last. I counted. It hurt, worse than any period or breaking a bone, which were my chief experiences with pain then. The violence of it shocked me, left me limp. In the recovery room I lay white and slack as an old flower. My head lolled to one side then the other as I saw the other silent women in their beds, covered with white sheets. The old aphorism echoed, *You made your bed, now lie in it.*

I was too weak to get up. But I told myself that I would be stronger, that if ever I became pregnant again I would have the baby, no matter what. Even then, being young, unmarried, and short on cash, I knew I had the resources (a desire for children in the future, education, a supportive family) to raise a child. I had let myself down, catered to a lesser version of me than I wanted to be. Now, I felt weak again. But I had never taken back the promise (as I had others).

When my back hurt recently, X-rays showed arthritis on the midspine, indicative not of an overall degenerative process but of an injury that caused bone spurs to grow. A serious injury more than ten years ago, the doctor said. He pointed at the translucent shapes, ghostly barnacles on vertebrae. Had I been in a car accident, or fallen down stairs?

I shook my head. Then I slowly remembered that I had once been in a train derailment. After college graduation, outside Philadelphia. I had been sitting in the last car, which turned over on its side and got dragged. Though the seats wrenched off their metal moorings, and suitcases fell on us from the racks, and a woman from across the aisle flew into my lap so hard she cracked the window with her forehead, I was fine, I thought. We all were. When the train screamed finally to a halt, all of us passengers in the last car joined hands, picking our way single file along the slanted floor through dust and smoke, then crawled out one by one through a broken window, squeezing through the space between the tipped car and the ground. The next day I was surprised to catch sight of purple bruises up and down my back—I laughed at my unsightly purple butt. Getting on another train the next day, I cried in gulps and my hands shook as the conductor took my ticket. But then it was over. I had walked away. Only, I hadn't. I had carried the accident with me, in my spine, for almost twenty years. While the doctor explained the X-ray, I thought, wonderingly, *Goddamn*, you really *can't* escape your past.

I had carried my abortion with me, too, a decision in itself that reflected so much else carried from the past, the conception of who I was and what I would become, and of how that would be made manifest. I was not the *kind of person* who would be pregnant at her college graduation. My father's photograph of me shows my hair cut newly short under the mortarboard, a dreamy happiness on my face as I held the rolled-up diploma. I was happy, free to move on, work full time, earn money, apply to graduate school and go there, where I would meet my future husband. But it turns out that in all that forward motion—as I cut off the past like my long hair, moved to the middle of the country and then the west, determined to follow every chance, have no regrets—there was, all along, an inner derailment, a refusal to move on without remembering.

When I arrived at Gettysburg College, people were still talking about the Peterson case. Brian Peterson, a Gettysburg College freshman, had gotten his girlfriend, a University of Delaware freshman, pregnant the previous fall. They had told no one, and when she went into labor on November 12, 1996, he drove from Gettysburg to Newark, Delaware, where the couple checked in to the Comfort

Inn, and she delivered a baby boy. He stuffed the baby into a trash bag and discarded him in the hotel dumpster, where he was discovered dead two days later. Peterson was serving a seventeen-month prison sentence in Delaware. Brian Peterson was a nice kid, professors said, and they wished they had known he was in trouble. Peterson's high school soccer coach was quoted in the Delaware *News Journal* as saying that Peterson must have told prosecutors the truth during the investigation, because "that's the kind of person he is." In the newspapers and on campus, people said, *How awful that Peterson and his girlfriend had killed their baby, how unimaginable.* But couldn't it be imagined? We all knew that secret mess, and the nightmarish feeling of the day of reckoning arriving for which one is unprepared ("He died suddenly, but not unprepar'd," one of my ancestor's gravestones reads, a hopeful sentiment).

My students here have written of their pregnancy troubles, after the fact. One wrote of leaving school for a semester to have her baby, conceived with the longtime boyfriend she loved. She had a healthy baby boy. Pressured by her boyfriend's parents, they gave up the baby for adoption, and in the moment of handing him over in the hospital corridor, she realized her heart was broken. And it was, I thought, but didn't say. Gazing at her bland blondness, reading her concluding words that she wanted "everything to go back to normal," I knew that wish, and that it would and would not be granted. In the semester I got pregnant, a student wrote of taking his girlfriend to get an abortion (I took notes—where? how?—while laughing grimly at myself). They felt sure about the decision, but sad. Their baby was due in August, too, just like mine. So now, when I carry my baby heavy on my hip, occasionally I think of my student, and that his baby would be the same age. How he'll carry that decision with him for the rest of his life.

Supposedly a Confederate soldier in rags skulks among the boulders of Devil's Den, where blood ran in creeks along the rocks. In various Gettysburg houses, shadows flicker on the walls, stairs creak, doors won't stay shut. Moans come from a field where a North Carolina brigade was buried in a long trench, as they fell in their marching line, and the grass, it is said, grows greener there. On campus, sentinels still watch the battle from the cupola of Pennsylvania Hall, and in the basement surgeons perform amputations. On Little Round Top, a Confederate officer on horseback picks his way downhill on moonlit summer nights. Whether the past is real and alive in this way I do not know. Our conceptions haunt us, idea-ghosts made visible, demanding to be claimed.

So I claimed my unexpected third child, deciding one day to be pregnant and happy about it. I celebrated by buying maternity tights and a soft knit baby cap. We named him Benjamin, a name we liked that occurred in both of our family trees. The hospital wouldn't release him without the full name on the birth certificate, and it was the middle name we agonized over, because we wanted to honor Kathryn. Finally we hit on Harvey, an adventurous uncle on my husband's side who had traveled Europe by motorcycle right after World War II, whose spirit seemed similar to hers. There were Harveys in my family tree, too. Thus Benjamin Harvey Leebron was given to our care. And Benjamin (the bundle in the picture, held tenderly, the promise of the future) truly is the last gift.

Sanguine

Right in town, in the Gettysburg Hospital, stands a well-equipped, permanent room especially designed for drawing blood. It's called a lab. But no one can afford to use it. Instead we all line up in one or another taxpayer-funded nonmedical site to get our arms stuck.

It costs thirty-two dollars for the usual screen, plus ten dollars for thyroid, or PSA or B-12. The blood drawing used to be held at the local rec park building. Now it's at the county emergency services building, outside of town on a brand-new winding country road. They could just as well draw blood at the public library, or firehouse, or agricultural center—any large room usable for voting, or the traveling reptile show, could be set up for phlebotomy.

I've had my blood drawn in a lab attached to a medical suite, or in a hospital, or at an off-site location attractive for proximity or shorter waiting times. Those labs all resembled each other in their hospital décor, their magazine-enhanced waiting areas and nurse-like receptionists, their blood drawing chairs set next to tables crowded with tubes. Fainters could opt for a bed or gurney with a pull-around curtain. I used to be a fainter, but then I ran out of time for the process of losing and regaining consciousness. So I started chatting up the phlebotomists while staring fixedly at an opposite wall, and remained upright.

Last time I had my blood drawn at the hospital lab, routine stuff requisitioned by my internist, the bill came to two hundred dollars, even with my semi-expensive employee-subsidized health insurance. My doctor waxed sympathetic, but, hey, he got his own testing done in the community multiphasic screen. My doctor lined up at the rec park? I imagined his friendly bespectacled face and white coat as he stood patiently in line by the playground.

So I signed up for the same, fasted ten hours, and drove five miles to park, at 7:15 a.m., in a large crowded lot with everybody else. I brought my memories with me, to contrast with the new era. There was a line out the door. A greeter checked my name off a list in the lobby, and gave me the lowdown. She pointed to a room beyond the lobby. "They'll give you your tubes in there," she said, "and there's food for after." Give me my tubes? Not to sound squeamish, but I'd never handled my own test tubes. I proceeded to a table lined with women in T-shirts and cardigans presiding over a cashbox, to pay forty-two dollars. They might have been working the school bake sale, a recent occupation of mine. I recognized their upturned smiling faces, their pleasure at exact change. They directed me to tables scattered with pens to fill out a form, as if I were registering my kid for youth soccer, which occurs in an elementary school cafeteria, and which would, apparently, be a fine place for the town's populace to sit down and get stuck with needles.

Form completed, I headed for the inner chamber, and another table of smiling women. A registrar studied my form, grabbed two plastic test tubes with rubber caps, and carefully penned my name and identifying numbers on the label of each one. Then she handed me my tubes and directed me to stand in line. Four long tables were being used for the testing, with metal chairs pulled up by the ends. Boxes of medical supplies filled all of the table space. The lab techs, all female and dressed in patterned scrubs, looked harried, rushing from here to there, brushing strands of hair back toward ponytails. Who signed up for this shift, I wondered, administering community blood tests from 6:30 until 8:30 a.m. without pause. These must be the newest or worst phlebotomists. A tall, unsmiling woman snapped off her blue gloves. I hoped I didn't get her. She raised a hand to summon me.

"Is there an arm you'd prefer?" she asked nicely. She had me sit in the appropriate chair and admired my visible veins. She had weird hair, a cap of blond wavy stuff rimmed at the forehead with flat cinnamon bangs, but now she looked me in the eye and smiled. "I bet you're ready for coffee, huh," she said. We chatted. She had this chatting thing down. Within a minute she knew that I was a college professor/writer with kids, and I knew that she was "an orange on the color wheel." Orange signified a creative type, according to her boss, the woman who supervised this bloodletting factory and who also happened to teach a class about the color wheel. "How do you know which color you are?" I asked.

"You take the class," she said. "There are four colors, orange, gold, blue, and green. If you know your color, then you can figure out how to get along with other colors. You must get some odd students, right?"

Affirmative.

"So you would learn how to interact with them. Like for me, I learned about golds, who are really moral. I'm in a gray area with that, but if I know they're golds and I'm orange, I can get along fine."

Mulling the concept of there being only four colors on the wheel, I felt relieved to hear about the gray areas.

"Nonfiction, there's nothing better than that," she remarked. "My mom gave me this *Good Housekeeping* contest to do, 2,500 words or less but it had to be fiction, and I was like, what? I don't want to make it fiction, I want to write about real life! You know?"

"Yeah. My husband writes fiction."

"Is it based on real life?"

I nodded. We both shrugged. "I know," I said. "I'd rather put my name on it and call it nonfiction." This comment represented a gross simplification, but I was following the phlebotomist's lead in the creative art of chatting. Who knew we would be discussing writing? I thought of this woman's mother handing her the contest clipping, encouraging her daughter's talents. She was a creative type, an orange on the color wheel, sugar dreams arrayed before her like a gummy-candy buffet.

"I had this great English professor, she let us go all out, do whatever we wanted, you know, where other teachers would always be telling you, you have to say it this way or whatever." She sighed. "I chose between writing, phlebotomy, and the whole medicine thing." I would have asked why—the obvious answer being financial—but our time was up. My phlebotomist had drawn my blood, skillfully, performing an intimate transaction. And she had also looked me in the eye, and seen me, and engaged in a real conversation. I don't know many people who can perform even the metaphysical part of her task, especially in less than five minutes.

I had much to ponder. I passed up the free blood pressure test and the foil-topped cups of orange juice and the cellophane-wrapped muffins. Call me a snob, but I had brought a Kashi brand granola bar. Was it to distinguish myself from the mobs who would grab at the crackling wrappers of low-quality free food? Or was it to preserve a measure of simple control over my choices while shuffling along with the masses?

After the last of us had passed the muffin display, the community blood-screening show would pack itself up, its needles and sharps containers, its tubes and labels, and head over the green hills to another county, vampiric peddlers, selling us clues to the mysteries of our own blood.

The Last Word

"Do I ever write, even here, for my own eye?
If not, for whose eye?"
—Virginia Woolf, *A Writer's Diary*

After my sister-in-law died, her husband, my husband, and I hunted through her house in London for personal writings. With the house empty of her, we were surrounded by sudden artifacts: her soft blue shawl over a chair back, her last painting on an easel in the kitchen.

She had wanted to write a memoir of her time with cancer (four and a half years, it turned out). Pain, weakness, and the pursuit of treatment had prevented her from writing a full manuscript, but we knew she had written pieces of her story. She had written the first chapter in a memoir workshop I taught for a week in the summer on Cape Cod, several years before. A vice president at Banc Suisse, she had written of becoming fluent in Chinese and Mandarin, of traveling in South America, and of one of the odd places she had arrived, a stone circle healing ceremony in upstate New York, as a forty-year-old cancer patient.

Her literary mentor of sorts, I led the hunt. We searched computer files and drawers, finding a couple of chapters, some short typed meditations, and several diaries, handwritten in spiral notebooks. Her husband, my husband, and I sat down on the living room couch with this cache of treasure: now we would know what she was thinking.

Not that she was unforthcoming in person—but writing, especially one's private writings, are supposed to be the truest record, untainted by social manners. In her diaries we would discover the faithful chronicle of an inner life.

Within an hour I had changed my mind. While the two memoir chapters possessed coherent narratives and complete ideas, and the short meditations reflected joyfully and descriptively on travels and healing ceremonies, the spiral-bound diaries portrayed a different mood. The diaries cast little lightning bolts of blame and anger around the family. As I read, I dreaded seeing my name. Lucky me, I wasn't important enough. The blood relatives suffered sharp shots of criticism—everything from helping to cause the cancer, to having the wrong values in life, to being selfish and inconsiderate. The diarist became a posthumous Zeus, casting judgments down as if from the heavens. I wished we had not found these notebooks, this turquoise half-script writing that expressed Kathryn so forcefully. Typed words possess a measure of cool distance. Handwriting evokes the pulse of the person writing. Handwriting gave us Kathryn—in the back garden, notebook on knees as she sat in a chair on the square of green lawn, or at her desk in the study she had painted sunflower gold—thinking these terrible thoughts. What is read can't be unread.

Having read a number of published diaries, and kept one myself, I summoned the few comforting ideas that came to mind. People often write diaries only in certain moods. Some people write when they're angry, others when they're depressed—in many cases, a strong feeling impels them to pick up the pen. Yet they don't *always* feel those feelings. The diary is only a partial record of their feelings on any subject. I said these things to her husband and to mine, who was her baby brother after all, trying to soften the blow. As Virginia Woolf commented about her own diary, "It is unfortunate for truth's sake that I never write here except when jangled with talk. I only record the dumps and dismals and them very barely." Kathryn found writing at all a major effort, and clearly it was anger that caused her to uncap the turquoise pen. Who wouldn't be angry, diagnosed with stage IV breast cancer at age forty? Still, her words devastated my husband. He and she had been close, both rebels and travelers. They had camped out on rooftops in Greece, and toasted the New Year together on rooftops in New York. His beloved sister was dead. Her last words about him, not last by date but last because they lasted as a written record, were unkind.

I used to be an avid diary reader. In my twenties, I collected Anaïs Nin's prodigious output, dating from 1914 until 1974, one volume at a time, pouncing on them in used bookstores. My husband, then boyfriend, didn't approve of their prominent display on our shelves—Nin wasn't literary enough, and her writing was self-indulgent, self-promoting, selfish. Her valuation of the self fascinated me, though, and her devotion to "the secret womb of the diary, the only laboratory of the truth." Writing before the era of copy machines and computer disks, Nin would finish a volume of the diaries and trundle it off to a bank vault. (While I kept all of my notebooks in a drawer wherever I lived, I didn't presume they warranted a fireproof, locked box in a federally insured building.) Along with reading Nin, I read diaries by May Sarton, Sylvia Plath, Virginia Woolf. I read the Tahitian journals of Paul Gauguin. I read collections of diary excerpts by contemporary Americans (collected in various categories such as African-American women, or poets), and I read the diaries of Christopher Columbus and of Cabeza de Vaca, Spanish explorer of the Americas in the 1530s. No other literature felt so visceral to me as these records of lived days, bound by time. The essay, memoir, poem, short story and novel might be written over any number of days and years. Only the diary reflected our existence in time, the condition we couldn't escape. A person wakes, thinks, writes, lives. Then the day is over. The day's thinking is over.

The modern-day diary has several origins—in pragmatic records such as ships' logs and household account books, in explorers' journals, and in Renaissance commonplace books, the collections of notable quotes kept by the educated classes of Europe. In the diaries we keep, often the day's mundane reckoning converges with the transcendently philosophical. We account for the day, and our consciousness of it. On reading diaries, I feel the force of emotion in the moment—*not* recollected in tranquility. I feel the painfulness of time in half-finished thoughts. I feel the urgency of the quotidian—so many biscuits eaten by the crew, so many goats observed on the hiking trail. I feel the sense of my own life—my desires, their fragmentation, and my need to give an account of myself: today I read such-and-such a book, did the laundry. Why? Why record all of this stuff?

In my case, the desire to chronicle must have begun after reading *The Diary of a Young Girl*, in the fifth grade. In a flowered, fake-leather, gilt-edged diary with a brass lock, I recorded secrets: how much I hated my teacher, who enjoyed humiliating me to tears; how I wanted my boyfriend to lead me into the woods behind school and kiss me. I was no Anne Frank. A crude line drawing of my teacher is captioned with a list of curse words that I was forbidden to say aloud. The diary served as repository. What I recorded later in my teenage years seems now so idiotic that I wish I hadn't written down anything. Whereas I might have looked back and assumed I had always been *me*, the diaries shoved a stupid self in my face, a girl who cared too much about being invited to the party, about which clothes to wear, a girl who bragged about drinking and defensively set forth the minor and major betrayals of high school life. I seem to have been a girl who had no mind of her own, although the very fact of a diary would seem the proof of an individual mind.

One day, in my thirties, after I had made the mistake of reading my old diaries, I saw four teenaged girls riding an escalator together at the mall. They were dressed alike, and all had highlighted hair, sparkly makeup. They stood bunched together, giggling and snapping their gum. And I thought, you are all exactly as stupid as you look. This observation disturbed me for its meanness, and also because I had harbored a myth about myself, that while I had looked and acted like a conventional, superficial teenaged girl, I had harbored a covert intelligence. But if the intelligence was not to be found in my diaries, then where was it? While I had conferred the knowingness of a later self upon an earlier one, the written evidence suggested otherwise. Yet when I wrote those diaries, I had intended to express my *truest self*. If the true self cannot be found in language, then where does it reside?

A child's point of view cannot be accurately rendered by a child. Only the adult, looking back, can create that perspective with any degree of wholeness. So, too, does the diary suffer from its habitation in the moment. The diary stubbornly refuses to gloss, to say, *They lived happily ever after*, or *Everything happens for a reason*, or *Those were the good old days*. The diary refuses finality, summary, and nostalgia. The diary is about the *now*. Sarton writes, "What delights the reader in a journal is often minute particulars." The diary in fact has no omniscient point of view, no god looking down from a hole in the sky. Diaries are written from the ground up.

"A great part of our life is an invention to avoid
confrontation with our deepest self."
—Anaïs Nin, *The Diaries of Anaïs Nin*

As I get older, I lose courage, and think of my teachers who kept their courage, kept opening themselves. Much of my life is a constructed shelter against chaos and discomfort, both physical and metaphysical. I could say I create an oasis in which to think. Or I could refer to Sarton, who writes, "Perhaps one must always feel absolutely naked and abandoned and desolate to be ready for the inner world to open again. Perhaps one has to dare that . . ." Do I not dare that anymore?

Maybe my sister-in-law Kathryn, desolate as she willed herself to live, dared that. And I, her doppelgänger in name, the so-called writer, do not dare anymore.

Sarton writes that the artist's "whole life is a painful effort to turn himself inside out, and if he gives too much away at the shallow level of social intercourse he may lose the will to attempt a deeper excavation." I volunteer at the elementary schools, chatting with other parents as we cut up oranges and lay them on a tray. Waiting in the lobby to pick up our children, we talk about birthday parties and allergies. In the yard I consult with neighbors about health matters, rosebushes, dogs. I like all of these conversations, which occur in a small town that has required me to concoct, and present, a whole self, a self that has perhaps become dangerously seamless and superficial.

We bought our first house (a brick house, impervious to wolves) in this town, and soon after moving in, we mentioned to our next-door neighbors that we were leaving for a two-week trip. Upon our return, people up and down the street and around the block greeted us with, "How was the Midwest?" How sweet—and yet I didn't even know their names, whereas they knew all about our travel plans. I wanted to hide. How exposed we were, in our house on the corner, with an unfenced yard. Every night at dark, I still lower all of the blinds, so the dogwalkers and strollers can't see in.

How I miss the anonymity of cities. If a person could see into a window of our fourth-floor walkup apartment in San Francisco, what did it matter? We knew only two of the thirty residents of our building. Hundreds of people lived on our block. Hundreds more streamed in and out of Golden Gate Park at the corner. Theoretically, I could run across the street to the Shell station for a Chipwich in my pajamas, and no one would care.

My husband and I lived in one other small town together, but it was the artists' and writers' community of Provincetown, Massachusetts, a place where "deeper excavation" was the point. Norman Mailer jogged slowly past our house every morning, puffing, his cloud of white hair a flag for the cause. In my conservative and rural Pennsylvania town, the familiar need to be obedient and admired kicks in—but at the shallow level. Come late September, I place pots of mums on the front stoop, followed by pumpkins, then dried corn for the brass door knocker, then a wreath—just like other women all over town. I cover the gray in my hair. I wear lipstick to PTO meetings, take my collapsible Walmart chair to soccer games, and smile brightly with little reason.

Shortly after we arrived here, my husband's sister received her diagnosis of metastasized breast cancer. The news came suddenly (her only symptom was back pain), and meant that my husband and I would visit her immediately in London. I would wean my son from breastfeeding (do you see how I can't resist including this detail to show that I am a *good mother*) to do so, etc. When the other mothers at the elementary school asked how I was, I told them. Then I understood that I shouldn't have. Behind their kind concern was a wall I would never breach: I wasn't from here, and I would never really know them. Years after that moment, I know from experience that one doesn't easily cross a threshold into these womens' homes. They stand politely, firmly, in the foyer of mine when we exchange our children after sleepovers. Maybe a small town is so intimate that decorum must be upheld, whereas in an artists' community or city, transience and anonymity mean that friendships can be more freely made and broken.

A woman from a small town once commented to *The New York Times* that as an antiwar protester, she had a harder lot than an urban protester; when *she* went home from the peace march in her town, everyone knew exactly where she lived. How many people know that I live in the brick house with blue shutters across from Eisenhower Elementary? Our attorney does—and he plays tennis with my husband. My real estate agent does—and our sons play on the same baseball and soccer teams. My daughter's friend's mother does—she and I once waited at the hospital lab together to get bloodwork done, she to test for cholesterol, me for gestational diabetes. Most people would say this chummy state of affairs was *nice*. At least no one is a stranger here. We're all snared in the community net of occupational, domestic, and leisure pursuits. We take care of each other, bringing casseroles for births and deaths.

But the small-town situation encroaches on the sensation of privacy. It ruins the illusion that one could have previous lives, or a work life and a home life, or a secret life and a public one. I present a seamless self as I walk from home to work, shop at the supermarket, take my kids to the pediatrician, teach class, and go out for coffee. I might as well pin my curriculum vitae, my "course of life," to my back. My persona is working mother, good mother, mother who volunteers at school, professor who is always prepared, professor who is always available to her students, wife (to bad-boy husband who writes nasty novels about marriage and small-town life, for which I both scold and applaud him, the twin impulses irreconcilable), woman who dresses neatly, shows up on time, smiles. You won't catch me yanking a child's arm too hard, or losing my temper at a faculty meeting. I'm pristine. Untouchable. Controlled.

What room is there for a writer in this persona? Where did she go? In fact, as I progressed through the tenure process in an academic department, I became ever more fearful. I said yes to every committee assignment. I felt embarrassed about my work, which lacked the sinew of serious research and focused on degraded subjects such as motherhood and mental illness. When the provost told me I would have to "make a case" for the value of the personal essays I had been publishing in glossy magazines one year, I crumbled further. (Having started out as a poet, I felt thrilled to see my work for sale in the supermarket—and I could now give you a tedious defense of its value to my students.) If I had once loved "The Love Song of J. Alfred Prufrock" for its lyricism, I now felt its middle-aged shiver: "And indeed there will be time / To wonder 'Do I dare?' and 'Do I dare?' / Time to turn back and descend the stair, / With a bald spot in the middle of my hair—"

In my previous lives I had maintained a secret self, my writing self. This self kept a diary. This self was accountable to no one, and, upon winning a high school prize for writing, was praised for "soul-baring poetry." As of age eighteen, because I lived in cities, or other countries, this writing self lived freely at home, and could even venture forth unnoticed to observe life comfortably as an outsider, a Woolfian street haunter. Who would notice my thrift shop clothes, or which book I was reading on the bus? Wherever I worked, I was the good girl—the skilled and cheerful waitress, housekeeper, file clerk, proofreader, tutor, researcher, editor, travel writer, adjunct instructor—and then I would come home and strip off those official clothes and breathe. It was not that I was shooting heroin at night, but simply that my mind was free.

Now I worry that this writing self has all but disappeared. I wear my proper clothes. I do not strip them off. There is no alter ego. I worry if my house is a mess, or if the grass grows too long. (My neighbors use edgers and trimmers and whackers.) While I eat lunch at my desk at work, I review proposals, peruse industry newsletters, and write recommendation letters. I read books that keep me current in my field. This succumbing to the status quo (with all of its attendant perks) feels insidious. Every couple of months, when my husband and I sit out on the breezeway late at night together we talk about our hopes and dreams—writing projects, or a plan to become expatriates. Shreds of a former self.

When *The Stepford Wives*, about men replacing their wives with domestic goddess robots, was remade, columnist Maureen Dowd pointed out that, "In the long interval between the two movies, women have turned themselves into Stepford Wives." The phenomenon included working wives: "Hillary Clinton, once so angry about tea and cookies, is now so eerily glazed and good-natured that she would be the Senator from Stepford." This seems a terrible truth. I have turned *myself* into a cupcake-bearing co-chair of the PTO and tenured English professor.

How do I turn back? How do I uncap my turquoise pen, to write things that—however uncharitable, half-finished, or even less than wise—express a real thought? Did my sister-in-law Kathryn ever imagine us going through her papers on the living room couch? The dead have no privacy. Did she care? She didn't stop writing. Her diaries upset us. Yet I admire her. She refused to embody the conventional ideal of the noble dying woman (she never complained, she took it in stride, she always thought of others before herself, she was a saint). It occurs to me that if everyone took misfortune and injustice "in stride," we would have no literature.

William Styron knew he intended to commit suicide when he planned to dispose of his notebooks. There would be no unkind or unfinished or private thoughts for the living to pick over, no little bones of his dead self. Moreover, the notebooks were him, or, as a writer, he was no more than what he wrote. The death of his notebook signaled the death of *him*. Now that I have stopped keeping a notebook I wonder if, in the most essential way, I am dead.

Ironing

Up in the Siberia known as Connecticut, oldest child's off-campus house may actually receive a generator today, and thus light, heat, and plumbing, in the wake of a blizzard. She has been camping out on the library floor, or in her freezing, dark house, for a week and I've been worrying. I feel as if my power will be restored as well.

Now feels like a good time to pick a word or a phrase, something short, and go after it, using the available equipment of intellectual retrieval, to see where we get.

That's Nicholson Baker beginning his essay, "Lumber," in *The Size of Thoughts*, and I like his thinking. Hauling out the *Oxford English Dictionary* and magnifying glass in search of "iron," I breeze by all sorts of great words, like "furze," "gunnery," and "insidiator," and keep on going. The other day I ironed for the first time in a while, and I wonder how long people have been using a hot iron to smooth out clothes.

"Iron" has a long entry. The word came into its present form in 1630, and clearly a lot of people have spent lifetimes tracking its phonetic and written origins through the British Isles while in the meantime other people were busy using the actual stuff mixed with carbon, in the forms of wrought iron, cast iron, and steel. That's a long way back from the electric iron I used in high school. I must have chosen the chore of ironing, as we had a non-dictatorial household (though I did not appreciate having to vacuum with a hangover!), and it seemed like a good choice. It was a meditative task that I could do while watching TV. I set up the ironing board in the living room in the evening, turned on a show (like *Three's Company*, or *One Day at a Time*, sitcoms that fed my apartment-dwelling aspirations), and set to it. Over time, it seemed like my mother and sister required that more and more of their garments be ironed. Hadn't we been content with minor wrinkles in the past? Probably I just fell behind, because I'm lazier than I imagine myself to be. So there would be a laundry basket heaped with blouses, blazers, and even pants.

In this era, people like to say carelessly, "I don't iron." It is much cooler not to iron, apparently. (They may not iron, but do they go to the dry cleaners? I don't ask.) I like wrinkled linen a lot, and I like covering wrinkled shirts with a cardigan and smoothing down the front with my hands. I grab clothes out of the dryer and drape them over chairs to prevent wrinkling. I will do a lot of work to avoid ironing.

But the other day, opening the dryer, I confronted a snarled tangle of shirtsleeves, like a netful of squid tentacles, created by my husband. He likes to stuff as much laundry into a machine as the machine can possibly hold. He does not turn socks, underwear, or shirts right side out before he washes them. When transferring from washer to dryer, he heaves huge wet lumps of clothes into the front-loader, not imagining that detangling might be wise. In fact, recently I hovered in the kitchen waiting for the washer to be done so I could transfer the clothes, and he caught me. "I'll transfer the laundry," he said, tapping on his iPad. I didn't think of anything plausible, like, "I need to pull out my bra and hang it up." No, instead I looked guilty. This was one of those representative moments of our marriage. Years ago—Portugal, 1987—I sliced a wedge of cheese for a picnic lunch in a spot of sun on the front stoop of a damp, chilly rented house. We had a really nice lunch. Actually we weren't married yet, and we were engaged in reading serious novels by Stendhal, and watching the film of *Death in Venice* on a tiny black-and-white TV, and going out for cheap food like sardines grilled on top of barrels. It was our high-intellectual period. The next day, I took out the cheese for lunch again, and there was my boyfriend, hovering. "I'll do this," I said, and he made a helpless gesture with his hands but also indicated that he would like the slicing knife. It came out that he thought the cheese should be sliced differently, and he had thought it the day before, but hadn't said anything. I was actually furious. "Were you privately criticizing the way I sliced the cheese?" I said. All of these actions were offensive to me: that he was critical, that he had withheld his critical opinion, and that he was fussy about cheese-slicing. And lo, these many years later, I was caught privately criticizing the way he handled laundry. High intellectualism is unsustainable.

The other day I hadn't intervened in laundry. According to the current culture, wifely scolding is a chief reason for husbands not doing more chores, and so I try to desist. I met that squid-tentacled tangle of shirtsleeves with brio: I would iron. According to one of my mantras, I wouldn't complain. The mantra is: if it takes less than ten minutes, don't complain about it, just do it. This mantra gets me through all manner of husbandly lapses in taking out garbage, changing lightbulbs, and emptying the basement dehumidifier. I got out the iron, and now it had a sweet, nostalgic quality. Middle child Jacob wears a button-down shirt most days now. He likes tweed blazers. (Unbeknownst to us all, he was dressing as the private prep school student he would soon become.) I knew he would appreciate smooth front plackets and sleeves. Just as in high school, I ironed school shirts, and office shirts, putting them on hangers, and in the end I felt content. Our world was orderly.

We live in a time between the promised knitwear of "The Jetsons" and buckskin. There's a lot of cotton still involved in my wardrobe. Youngest child is future-oriented, wearing T-shirts and jeans (though he recently declared, "I'm a khakis person," so I may be wrong). He proposed that toweling off after a shower was annoying, and that there should be a whole-body dryer. We mused upon a car wash-like device that would wash and dry a person fast. I thought of the logistics of loading it up with my highly specific products, full of volumizers and color preservers and microscrubbers, but youngest child uses only one product—a squirt bottle of SpongeBob all-purpose washing liquid—so these nuances bored him. Ironing, like childbirth, is still a primitive task, though well along the human history timeline as far as implements. In the *Oxford English Dictionary*, the linen-smoothing sort of iron appears in definition number five, past tools and guns and whaling harpoons, showing up in 1613, as box-iron, flat-iron, and Italian iron. In 1840, Dickens describes a female character as coming to the fireplace for another iron. My plug-in iron is more advanced than the flame-heated sort, though still simple, as I press heated metal along a length of cloth. The iron is reassuringly solid and finite, in an uncertain world. As I ironed, Benjamin posited that without colors, it would be a dark world; without colors, the world wouldn't exist. To which Jacob replied, "How do you know? Animals don't perceive color the way we do. How do you know *colors* exist?" Between blizzards and such philosophizing, we have little to cling to.

Ironing is a luxury, of course. No one irons in an emergency. I bet the rate of ironing in Connecticut has fallen to record lows.

Nota Bene

"Fern" can be slang for "butt," which I just learned from an essay on slang by Nicholson Baker, as in, "You know, the hardest part of all this is the feeling of sitting around on our ferns, doing nothing." I won't think of my kitchen windowsill fern plant in quite the same innocent way.

N.B. Shall I retitle this piece "My Love Affair with Nicholson Baker?" Maybe not. But his thoughts have a way of hanging around in my head. For example, he doesn't appreciate new compound words (livingroom, backseat) and would strongly prefer that hyphens were used. Re-title might find favor with him.

Recently I was wondering whether the implosion of Borders and Barnes & Noble would result in the library becoming the last place one could go to look at books in the paper flesh, to hold them, and turn them over and heft them and flick through their pages. I love to browse in the library, by standing in front of actual bookshelves to find the book I came for, and then reading the titles all around it. And libraries have obscure and out-of-print books—would I find all of Anne Carson's work in a glossy bookstore crammed with only the recent and the marketable, the temporarily anointed ones? Of course not. Scholars, not sellers, stock libraries. Yet according to NB, the content of libraries is in danger, heralded by the gleeful dumping of card catalogs in favor of software versions. He identifies a trajectory leading from library-as-repository to library-as-information-dispenser, via machines. This is worse than closed stacks! In a very long essay (one could doze off on the train and wake up to be in the middle of a large word forest), "Discards," NB enumerates the losses engendered by the transition to software (faulty, always misrepresenting a percentage of books, causing them to be invisible to searchers), and the wholesale tossing of intelligently annotated vanilla cards.

And, personally tragic for me, he claims that librarians hope for the day when "they will be able to define themselves as Brokers of Information and Off-Site Digital Retrievalists instead of as shy, bookish people with due-date stamps and wooden drawers to hold the nickel-and-dime overdue fines. . . ." Growing up as a girl with straight brown hair who loved to read books, I aspired to be a mousy librarian. I wished I had to wear glasses. Because then, after all, I would take down my hair, and take off my glasses, and be beautiful. Can we really dismiss such an enticing cultural model?

My mother wore aviators in the '70s and looked like powerful, beautiful Gloria Steinem, with her long hair middle parted, her hands on her hips. My sister got glasses early, and though she had to suffer through glasses-and-braces, when she reached college, she looked as intellectual as she was. When I finally earned distance glasses, it was just in time to live in Barcelona, where one of the female fashion paradigms involved skinny little glasses and a long shiny ponytail. The only nickname I'd ever had, really, was Pony (Camp Tohikanee, age twelve, nickname due to ponytail, I hoped, rather than buck teeth, too grateful to have been deemed nickname-worthy to investigate the matter), and I could manage the ponytail. Now I had the glasses, too! In a coffeeshop, writing in a notebook with a *cortado* at hand, I belonged. (The other fashion paradigms were impossible, anyway, requiring youth, beauty, or money.)

Every night while watching an episode of *30 Rock* I wear my glasses and smile at Tina Fey. However, rounder glasses are coming back in, so my paradigm is shifting. Glasses allow you to be at least two selves. Put them on, take them off. Stare down your nose through them.

Since the myth of the patient Sybil has been debunked, I wonder how greedily we wanted her to have sixteen different selves. A disturbed young woman named Shirley Mason entered therapy with Dr. Cornelia Wilbur in the 1940s, and the account of their sessions, published as *Sybil* in 1973, sold six million copies in the United States. According to Dr. Wilbur, and the book's writer Flora Schreiber, Mason had constructed a host of alternate selves as a way of dealing with merciless childhood abuse. Each "self" had a different name, voice, and personality, so that poised Vicky would speak in one psychiatric session, little Peggy Ann in another. One-fifth of all Americans saw the 1976 television movie based on her story (the image of the terrorized girl tied to a piano leg will not leave me!). Looking back, I wonder at how readily we accepted the whole scheme, that a person could be multiple. The term multiple personality disorder, or MPD, was given its own label four years after the movie *Sybil*, in the *Diagnostic and Statistical Manual of Mental Disorders III*, published in 1980, and in my teaching, I've worked with students who identified themselves as having it. One woman I'll call Donna would miss a college class and then appear at my office using a different voice to give her excuse: "Donna wasn't feeling well," a growling male voice would say. "Okay," I'd answer cheerily, as if this were a commonly understood way of operating. "Please tell her to follow the syllabus for Thursday." Another took a week-long summer workshop in the 1990s, along with her therapist, and though the diagnosis had become controversial by then, truly I was nearly as willing to believe in their cause as they were: a memoir featuring the vivid characters inhabiting the pleasant woman who occupied an ordinary desk chair. Working with multiple personalities was more exciting and creative than working with a single one—for me, for them, for all of us in the workshop, and apparently for wishful therapists. According to an October 2011 *New York Times* article by Debbie Nathan, Dr. Wilbur would tell the screenwriter of the Sybil story that, "This is one of the most outstanding cases of all time."

"I am all of them," Mason wrote to her psychiatrist in 1958. In a letter to Dr. Wilbur she said that she had been lying, that she didn't have sixteen personalities. She didn't even have a double, she wrote—she was just one person. But Cornelia Wilbur, for whom

Mason was a career-making patient, dismissed this claim as a defensive maneuver. It was more fascinating, amazing, and psychiatrically groundbreaking to believe in multiple personality disorder. And maybe it even bolstered the American faith in reinvention. A person could be one way today, and another tomorrow. A person could be one way during the day, and another way at night. The librarian is sexy because when she whips off those glasses and takes down her hair . . . watch out. Superheroes are often doubles—why should the rest of us have to settle for one identity?

I caught a glimpse of the mousy-haired girl I was on the train one day, as I rode from the city of New York back to the country of Pennsylvania, and passed the eternal bridge over the Delaware that says, "Trenton Makes, the World Takes." The sign meant to evoke industrial prosperity, but it always seemed sad to me, as if everything Trenton made was taken away. The sad interpretation fit the mood of Trenton as a city of want and need. Beyond the bridge, there on the Pennsylvania side, behind the screen of trees, was the girl of me; and this time she felt like a figure distinct from myself, a person far away. I was sitting on my fern. She was standing in the woods watching the river and I rode right on by and left her there. Bye-bye sweetie! Have a nice life!

In Transit

There is the birthplace, and there is the deathplace. We are in the deathplace. The deathplace is Bad Aibling, in Southern Germany, just north of the Austrian border. To get here, we have driven through the Tyrol, the Italian-Austrian-German alpine region in which gingerbread houses stack up on the green slopes of valleys.

Bad Aibling sounds fitting for a deathplace, a bad place, though in fact "*Bad*" means "bath." As we drive on a two-lane road, we see cars parked in bunches on the grassy shoulder, and it seems people might be bathing, dipping their feet in the country creeks the way it's done in Tuscany, where each creek is known for its particular qualities of minerals and temperature. I might bother to find out about creek bathing if I were a tourist, but I am not. We simply glide in suspension, the place of death acquiring properties as we approach. Bad Aibling is a spa town, and seemingly as an extension of the warm baths, clinics have arisen here. We are looking for the Klinik Schloss-Prantseck, at which patients receive hyperthermia, a superheating of the waters.

Schloss-Prantseck is hardly the only clinic, which becomes clear as each turnoff sprouts signs and arrows. My husband speaks German, so he asks directions at a gas station convenience store. His "*Guten Abend*," or "Good Evening," is met with "*Grussegott*," or "Greet God," the phrase of greeting, we learn, for everyone at all times of day and night in Bad Aibling. The townspeople here expect that the international clientele of the local clinics will acquire this basic civility and say "*Grussegott*" when entering a shop or restaurant. The greeting of one's supposed maker strikes me as a chilling custom for a place where the gravely ill converge, seeking a reprieve.

We follow the map but miss one turn, and my husband pulls over to ask a man walking a dog outside a housing development. The man smiles, gestures, and speaks at length while his golden dog bounds over the grass. He praises my husband's proficiency in German. It is good for this conversational moment to last, because we are still in suspension, whereas soon we will arrive. Though we have been driving fast—so fast that the Italian police pulled us over for speeding and we had to beg them not to confiscate my husband's license—my husband and I have always appreciated being in transit, driving in a car or stuck in a motel room between points A and B, between departure and arrival.

In the clinic parking lot we do not see our brother-in-law's car. We do not see the main entrance to the group of pink buildings. The sign over one door reads "*Bad Haus*" so we choose a different, larger building and walk in. We see no reception desk, and find ourselves in a library. *Chicken Soup for the Christian Soul* sits on a coffee table. When we had called the other night we couldn't talk to my husband's sister because she was "downstairs watching a movie." She must have been here, in the velour chair. I stare at it. I wonder what she watched, *Uncorked* or *The Other Sister*, or one of the other unremarkable American comedies lined up next to the television. She wasn't even watching anything good, her last movie. My husband uses a telephone in the library, which rings reception, and we learn that Mr. Smyth, our brother-in-law, is just upstairs in Room 121.

We find stairs under a sign marked "*Ausgang*." My husband and I do not like Germany. Exclamation points proliferate on road signs, and this characteristic, combined with the German words, makes everything sound like a concentration camp command. *Ausgang!* My husband is Jewish. I read Anne Frank early in life. We go up the German stairs.

Upstairs the place reveals itself as a hospital, with IV poles and a wheelchair in the hallway. The door to Room 121 is closed. A label in an acrylic holder outside the door reads "Mrs. Smyth." I wonder suddenly whether she will be in the room, lying on a bed. But of course she is not. Both single beds in the room are empty of her. The bed on the right is a work surface, covered with books, papers, and a telephone. Our brother-in-law opens his arm to the other bed. That is the one. He has pulled the white comforter up to two pillows. He has laid a purple knit cap on the pillow where her head was. Along the comforter he has laid in a row two small paintings. The painting on the left, called "Heart Swinging," is of a strong red heart rising out of dirt, a heart with black-and-white wings. Our six-year-old son Jacob painted this on Sunday. The thick paint took two days to dry. I mailed it on Tuesday. The painting on the right by our nine-year-old daughter Cade is called "Lavender Drying," showing three bunches of lavender hanging from a beam. It is a death image. But our brother-in-law Tim has turned the painting upside down so the lavender sprouts straight up. Today is Thursday. My husband's sister did not see the paintings because they arrived this morning, and she died last night, June 5, at ten o'clock.

There is certain information that is difficult to live with. Last night my husband and I decided to drive to the clinic, from southern France where we are living this year. Tim was sitting here, on the bed with the telephone. Kathryn lay in the other bed. Tim left the room to get us driving directions. He was gone for about five minutes. She died, alone, while he was out of the room.

Turns out we didn't need directions. We have found this place with a map and three conversations.

Later my husband will say he wanted to hug the bed. He wants to cross the room and open his arms to the bed where his sister died, but he does not. The three of us stand in the room looking at the bed. It is easier for one person to maintain control if the others do. Later we will sit on the floor with our backs resting against the bed, and later still we will sit on the bed that seems to thrum below our threshold of knowing. Now we look at this bed, at what it has all come down to, this single bed in the corner of a clinic room in Bad Aibling, Germany. I am endlessly self-consciously literarily historically philosophically aware that people die all the time, and many in worse circumstances than this. (We are in Germany after all.) I do not care. That quilt was rumpled by her, and she put that book on the bedside shelf, the novel she said was trashy but held her attention, at a time when few things could. She was here.

The birthplace will always be Philadelphia, and the deathplace will always be Bad Aibling. The mortuary wants to see her birth certificate to establish that Philadelphia was her actual birthplace, because her passport indicates only the state of Pennsylvania. Tim doesn't know where her birth certificate is, back at their house in London, so the mortuary agrees to go ahead and prepare the certificate. They will give Tim fifteen copies. Most people only need a few, but the Americans, they say, always want fifteen copies.

The mortuary still wants to see her birth certificate, as soon as possible, "for the file." My husband and I feel a Nazi chill at this meticulous posthumous filekeeping. They also need a marriage certificate, in order, after the cremation, to release the ashes to Tim. He doesn't know where it is, but my husband's mother finds a copy in Philadelphia, where they were married, and faxes it over.

The accuracy of the death certificate is essential, as is the telephone call to the United States Embassy in Munich and subsequent cancellation of her passport, because this is a moment when someone could assume her identity. Her official identity is in transit until the proper authorities are notified. Some other tall American woman in her mid-forties could become her.

This is also a moment of transit for the soul. Tim introduces us to Dorothy, who teaches Qigong at the clinic, does Reiki treatments, and is known as a psychic. (A skeptic, I have to say "is known as.") Dorothy says Kathryn's "luminous body" remains in her body for three days, which is why cremation should occur only after that time. The night Kathryn died, Dorothy sat with her after and "saw" a small ginger and white animal, she says. What is it, she asked Tim then—did Kathryn have a cat? She didn't. At that time, while Dorothy and Tim sat with Kathryn, my husband and I were on our porch in France, with our arms around each other. Our daughter's rabbit, named Ginger Blaze for his orange and white fur, hopped around and around us. He does this, the compulsive circles. Did Dorothy "see" the rabbit while sitting with Kathryn? Was Kathryn somehow seeing us? Was she with us there, was she thinking of our daughter?

There is certain information that is difficult to live with. At dinner Tim tells us that Kathryn wanted to see our daughter before she died. We are sitting outside at an Italian restaurant, with a view of blue mountains and an onion-domed bell tower. Bad Aibling is a picturesque town, with a butter yellow church, and decorative painting on the shop façades. My husband had talked to Tim at five o'clock the afternoon before, and said that we were driving up, and bringing the kids. After he hung up, he said that Tim had hesitated when he heard the kids would be coming. Why? Maybe it would be too overwhelming for her, the four of us coming? Maybe she would worry about the children seeing her so ill? They had just had a pleasant visit together. Maybe it would seem that she was going to die, if we all rushed up there for a deathbed scene? So my husband emailed and said we wouldn't bring them. Now, in the mild June air at the restaurant, we listen to Tim say that when Kathryn heard our daughter was coming, she perked up, she roused herself. The technical term for her situation then was "liver coma," or an almost complete failure of the liver. Her liver couldn't withstand the toxicity of the chemotherapy, which she was receiving along with hyperthermia. Still, there was a slight chance of reversal. To hear Cade was coming, she was happy. When Tim received our email and told her Cade was not coming after all, he says, she sank back down. My husband says nothing, tears in his eyes. We have seen the bed. I can imagine her pulling herself up higher on the pillows, then sinking back down into them.

"It was a mercy she died last night anyway," Tim says. "I couldn't have stood another night like the one before. No sleep, and her breathing was so labored."

We should have brought our daughter, I think. We should have at least *said* we were—anything to have kept Kathryn going. There was always a chance. I think of the last printout on our desk at home, about Apheresis, another treatment, "the next step," the doctor called it. I will hate that printout, I will crumple it up when I see it. The last treatment: expensive, experimental, and never to be.

There was always another plan, another medicine or poison or procedure or clinic or healing session. How many pages had we printed out, about Zoladex, tamoxifen, Quadramet, Pamidronate drips, Didronel I.V. infusions, Xeloda, Herceptin, Taxol, Fosamax, Arimidex? Or about alternative treatments—mistletoe, milk thistle, Chinese mushrooms, shark and bovine cartilage, and any number of teas, elixirs, and capsules. There were healing treatments, such as colonic irrigation, aromatherapy, iridology (mapping body function through study of the eyes), and there were clinics everywhere: for emotional/spiritual work in the Netherlands, say, or for deep purification in Wales. Then there were the printouts about experimental doctors: a Dr. Burzynski of Houston pushed antineoplastons, biochemical microswitches that "turn off" genes that cause cancer and "turn on" tumor suppressor genes; Dr. Simone of Lawrenceville, New Jersey, had appeared on *60 Minutes* and *The Today Show* to talk up ONCOR and CALCOR, his miraculous nutrient supplements; Dr. Moss of Brooklyn, upon perusing a patient's complete file, provided a personalized "Healing Choices" report; and Dr. Wolfgang Scheef of the Robert Janker Klinik, featured in *Esquire* and *Family Circle*, gave Interleukin-2 injections in Bonn.

Had I once, in the 1980s, shaken my head at newspaper stories of cancer patients traveling to Mexico for Laetrile? How pathetic they were. Laetrile was quackery. But I had changed. No plan was pathetic. A plan was a way to keep moving, maybe even forward. Interleukin-2 *was* Laetrile, with the innovation that Scheef injected it directly at the tumor sites. So one summer we met Kathryn and Tim in Bonn, where she received injections, and it did not feel crazy at all. We stayed at a Holiday Inn, where Jacob swam in the indoor pool, and we found a good Thai restaurant across the street, and we walked in the gray cold along the gray river where boats plowed relentlessly ahead, and in a beer garden golden ale bubbled in tall glasses. At a playground Cade found a porcelain star mounted on a stick, just lying there in wet sand, a magic wand. Maybe Interleukin-2 would be *just the thing.*

There was always another plan, we kept making plans, stretching a string out into the future and pinning it down on a date. But now we would not be together for a week in a rental house in July. And my daughter would not spend her tenth birthday with her Aunt Kathryn in London before we flew home to the States.

When she was first diagnosed in December 1997, the family mood was one of emergency. We spent Christmas arranging a second opinion at Memorial Sloan Kettering. They told her the initial diagnosis in London had been correct, that they had done a "good job" in London. She could live anywhere, they said, and pursue any treatment she wished—because nothing would work. She and Tim flew home to London. Her family mobilized. She had two parents, four married siblings. My husband and I flew to London in January. She lay on the couch, surrounded by stacks of cancer books. "My new library," she said ruefully. We considered moving to London. I had lived there twice before. But economics confounded us: quit our new jobs, sell our new house? Instead, we were on the phone, the Internet, the airplane. My father had just remarried, and my new stepmother the pilot gave us her companion passes so we could fly free, at the last minute, whenever we wanted.

Four and a half years is a long emergency. How much time passed until my attention wavered? I would get sick of the constant test results, the dread, the keeping track of clinics in the Canary Islands or China. China was the fourth summer. This would have been the fifth. I knew my attention wavered, and I judged myself weak on fortitude, mercy, and concentration. I let my husband carry the thinking for a week at a time. When did we stop toasting her every time we had a glass of wine? After the third year?

Now there would be no more parceling out of time and attention. No more checking the calendar to work around children's piano recitals or soccer games, or professional conferences and deadlines. Now suddenly everyone can get on an airplane, everyone can take off time from work, everyone can fly in to this little deathplace of Bad Aibling, even in the midst of business trips to Japan or Los Angeles.

"I told her, last night, that everyone was coming," my husband says, having wanted to assure her that her parents, her brothers, and sisters would all be by her side.

Tim laughs. "That's probably what did her in. I think she wanted to die alone."

In the morning, in the room, Tim is fumbling with a gray jewelry pouch, and then he has pieces of her jewelry in his hand. He says, "She wanted Cade to have this." I sit down in a chair beside him. He holds up the ring, and I can picture it on her hand, the large rectangular diamond flanked by sapphires. My four sisters-in-law all have large diamond rings. He kisses the ring, and swiftly presses it into my palm. I want to ask, *Are you sure*, but he has already made the hard gesture. Then he says, "Oh, you need something to put it in," and he comes up with a Ziploc bag. They used to be so precious, the Ziploc bags, you couldn't get them in London and whoever was flying over brought Ziplocs, to store medicines in the freezer. But there it is, a Ziploc bag, no need to hoard them anymore. I hate the sight of it. I drop the ring in, roll up the bag, and stuff it in my purse.

At first when my husband and I arrived, Tim asked us to help pack up the room but today at breakfast he didn't feel like it. In the room he has lit votive candles, three on the shelf alongside the bed. A low shelf between the two beds serves as a night table. Nearest her side are a collection of medicines, and new photos of her brother and his children from New York. (Ping took the pictures. She was like me: sister-in-law, wife of a brother whose sister was dying, maker of phone calls, sender of packages.) In the middle of the shelf Tim has constructed a shrine: a photograph of Gurumayi, their yoga guru, more candles, a Chinese silk snap pouch, a statuette of an elephant god or goddess, an incense holder. The room smells of incense. Chanting music uncoils out of the CD player. Tim is keeping the room going. He slept the night before in the bed where she died, I realize with a start, because the other bed hasn't been slept in. The trash cans are overflowing. Roses in a vase curl and brown. He wants nothing touched.

Tim says we can put something in the coffin when she is cremated. We will put in the photo of our two children, the one I carry everywhere in my wallet, the one that's good luck when I travel, the one I can whip out for the police officer when the children go missing, I can say: *There they are, they look like that.* My daughter with her long Botticelli hair wears a yellow T-shirt with a glittery star on the front. She is looking down because my son, with a mischievous smile, is elbowing her in the ribs. They are standing in front of our brick house, the very symbol of security. "We'll put in that photo," I tell Tim. "Cade and Jacob will be good company in the universe." But I am disturbed to think of burning, even burning that little rumpled photograph.

How unacceptable it is to conceive of my children's spirits accompanying their aunt on her disembodied journey. Just three weeks before, she had visited us, the first time in a year her vital signs were strong enough for airplane travel. It had been grimly dark and raining in Tourrettes-sur-Loup, weather that I usually like as it evokes the Middle Ages in the medieval town. The rain washes down the sides of the narrow stone street and empties in the ravine, just as it did five hundred years before. But Kathryn had come from London to the south of France for sun, and the slick street was difficult to negotiate. I held her arm as we walked slowly up to the square. She was frail now. She used to be solid; she had been the first woman basketball scholar at Georgetown University. In her old apartment in New York City, she had kept rollerblades and a bicycle stuffed in a closet, pulled out every weekend. When she visited us in San Francisco, she thought nothing of going out by herself to rent a mountain bike and ride over the Golden Gate Bridge. This impressed me, being the sort of person who reads a book for three hours and then takes a walk. On my honeymoon, I stared at the ocean a lot. On her honeymoon, she got helicoptered out to a glacier and skiied down.

In Tourrettes-sur-Loup on the stone street, I held her arm especially tightly on the uphill part. Her eyesight wasn't good anymore, for depth, or the subtle gradations of concrete and cobblestone. She kept her head bowed. The market had mostly closed early because of the rain. We looked at clothes. She bought cotton pants, good for the clinic, she said, because you have to go out for treatment, so you need to be dressed to receive the local and whole-body hyperthermia that supposedly shrank tumors. The treatment was painful, like being burned. I bought her a bright pink T-shirt to match the pants, with three-quarter sleeves and maroon piping. That is what the nurse dressed her in after she died. We went to the next stall. She bought me a jacquard dishcloth in orange and yellow. She admired the matching tablecloth, which would go well in her kitchen. She had no cash left. I had just enough. I didn't buy it for her. That is what I mean by the parceling out, the rationing, the stinginess. Two weeks later I bought it for her. I sent it to the clinic. My packages to her felt like good luck charms flung at the void. I kept busy, wrapping up olive oil soaps and paperback books, carrying them to the post office.

During her visit to us, my husband drove her down to the coast for lunch in Cannes and to see the fancy hotels where the celebrities would stay later in the month for the film festival. The marble floors of the Carlton Hotel lobby, she told me later, were so incredible, the wheelchair just glided. Smooth, she concluded appreciatively, the former basketball star praising the quality of a wheelchair ride.

When she died (why insist on such harshness, why not just say "passed away" as other people do, instead of thinking such clarity is *superior*), I stayed composed, for my husband. He had just talked to her an hour before. Our suitcases were packed to leave for Germany the next day, leaving at 5:00 a.m., so we wouldn't be driving the tunnels and mountains in the dark. My mother, visiting us for a month and renting a separate house, was sleeping over to take care of the kids and put them on the schoolbus. The kids were in bed, and my mother, husband, and I had just finished writing postcards at the table when the call came. Our daughter would be going on a school trip to the mountains the next week, and we were supposed to send cards for her to receive there.

You're always doing something when the call comes, of course. When the diagnosis call had come four and a half years before, I'd been on campus grading papers. It was a Saturday morning, but my husband had been away for a week and I was behind at work. He said to come home. I said why. He said, *Just come home.* Kathryn's mystifying back pain had been identified as metastasized cancer of unknown origin. It was December 20, 1997. Our son was one and a half, our daughter was five. It felt as if everything vertical and sturdy and upright in our lives—our first house, our new job, our sense of intactness—had been smashed flat. Our children must have wondered at their parents clinging to each other and crying, or maybe they just stared at their television show. Four and a half years later, when the call came, I stayed composed. It was ten o'clock. My husband made and received a number of telephone calls. The family was traveling to see her, his parents having canceled their fiftieth anniversary Caribbean cruise, one sister flying in from a conference in Los Angeles to travel with the other sister from Virginia, his brother en route from Tokyo to New York (his home, where Ping also stayed composed) to Munich. No one would see her now, sit at her bedside, hold her hands, say they loved her. They were all still coming anyway, converging on Bad Aibling like pilgrims.

I stayed composed until, dressing for bed, I saw our digital clock turn to 0:00. That is how the European clocks are, like military time, so that midnight is not twelve o'clock but the zero hour. It seemed cruel that the day was over, that it wasn't the day she had died anymore, the day when she was alive and might have kept on living. It was June 6, the day after, and people were already talking about the memorial service.

There are several things I want to say to her. I rehearse the main points silently as we walk up the mortuary driveway. *I didn't think it would come to this,* is one point, the pure and main point. There is a difference between hope and denial. She didn't want to be thought of as ill. A few days after diagnosis, she wrote to us, "I am scared and apprehensive, but my courage and conviction must let me rise above whatever comes my way." A day after that she stopped taking pain-killers and reported that she and Tim had gleaned what good news they could from a depressing doctor's appointment, and were elated to meet the challenges ahead. "If any of you," she wrote to the whole family, "think we're out in the clouds, keep it to yourself. I do not mean that to be harsh, but I cannot afford to have anyone near me who expresses doubt." Weeks later she had fixed on the philosophy that would carry her forward: "Bottom line I am not interested in hearing negative doom and gloom feedback." She wouldn't say she had a disease, except in deconstructed form: she had a dis-ease, she would say, an unease in her body. She mentioned her legal will several times over the years, but she wouldn't have wanted me to bring it up in conversation. We focused on the future—the next treatment plan, the next time we would see each other. We talked about books, and we liked to read the same ones together, but they couldn't include any of the characters having cancer. Characters with cancer are surprisingly prevalent in contemporary American fiction. The final two books we read together were historical novels about a British royal gardener. We talked about her family—her two parents, four siblings, four in-laws, three nieces and five nephews, as well as a number of cousins and their families—the psychodynamics and history of all of these living relatives, as well as various dead ones. I saved up funny stories about my children to tell her. Always I had to have them, so when something funny happened—like Jacob tackling our mother cat to try to breastfeed, or Jacob swallowing my silver teardrop earring, or Cade spying on the neighbor boy with binoculars—I was instantly storing it to tell her, like money tucked in a wallet. I played the foolish sister-in-law, always ready to gossip, sending the latest celebrity magazines over to London with my husband. She told me medical things when my husband wasn't home and she was too tired to call back later. I wrote down the particulars, to tell my husband, to email the family, and for research, and we put these notes and our research printouts in a brown expandable file, leaned casually against our printer table. The file will get no thicker.

From the beginning she did not want to hear prognosis.

Diagnosis, okay, but no prognosis. My husband and I researched prognosis and despaired, the median survival rate for metastasized breast cancer being two years. She was forty. She didn't want to hear prognosis, she wanted to strategize and move forward. The doctor in London said, *Put your affairs in order.* The doctor in New York said, *Start morphine.* She regarded taking morphine as succumbing to death. She took it rarely. On the last day of her life she refused to take it. My daughter had morphine as an infant; she flew through the death-night and came out. Even when Kathryn was well, she had loved my daughter for her life force.

I am walking up the gravel mortuary driveway with her husband and brother. I didn't think it would come to this. Tim has asked the undertaker to bring Kathryn outside, in the cloisters. The morning is rainy and the cloisters provide shelter. Tim says she was feeling "cooped up" inside, and needed fresh air. Also, he says, she didn't like the hum of a large appliance that could be heard in the inside viewing room.

She is in a wooden box, lying down of course. The box has no lid. Two mortuary guys in suits are standing with their hands clasped in front of them, at a distance from the box out in the courtyard. They nod and bow slightly. We nod and bow slightly back. It is stark to see her in the box. This is the only way she will look when she's dead; there are no other possibilities or contexts but these pale yellow arches and a gray light and her lying dead in our sight.

Tim takes off his jacket and camera and puts them on the ground. He kisses her forehead, her collarbone, her hands. I stay back. He visits her, then my husband does. I'm the outlaw here (a family nickname for the five of us who married in), so I stand back. I take two objects from my purse: her wedding ring, and the photo of my children. I want her to see them, or them to see her, or all of them to be present together—I don't know which. If ever I had a chance of being a rationalist, it was lost when my daughter survived. When she was born, her respiratory system failed, and the numbers were against her, both the medical statistics and the numbers on the monitoring machines. Several things might account for her living, and when I was told afterwards that an African prayer circle had been praying for her, I couldn't discount it. Now nearly ten years later I can listen to Tim say "she needs fresh air" about his dead wife and conclude that: she must need fresh air. The more we researched cancer over these years, the more the unknown outweighed the known, the mystery acquiring vastness and weight. If we were to conceive of it in the German philosopher Kant's terms, the nuomena, or the unknown, came to overwhelm the phenomena in our experience of the world.

She is wearing the pink knit cap I bought her in Saint Paul (deathplace of James Baldwin). She is wearing a white linen blouse she wore all the time. (She was wearing it one day in Périgeux, sitting on the grass with my husband, watching our children play in a fountain. She was smiling then, her teeth white, her brown wavy hair cut in a short bob.) Around her neck as a shawl is a hot pink pashmina. She believed in the warm colors, the healing colors. She is holding a pink peony in her lovely bony hands, clasped on her stomach. Below that she is covered by a white satin quilt, which must belong to the mortuary because it is coldly white and artificial. Red roses are laid here and there around her. This is all peripheral: I am looking at her face. Her mouth is open, there are her front teeth, and her bottom lip seems bitten and chapped. I didn't expect her mouth to be open. In the room, Tim had showed us a video he took after her death, in which she is lying flat on her back holding a flower, her mouth closed. I can't speak. If I had a chair I could sit down and chat, about how I didn't think it would come to this, and how she dignified me as a person by thinking well of me, and how generous she was, but I can't speak. I am clutching the ring, and showing her the photograph, and crying. I can't hold all of this sadness, what do people do with it. Stupid people have surmised that it is bearable for her parents to lose a child because they have five, or that it is expected and acceptable for her to die because she had cancer; and to them I want to say: Why is it acceptable that she had cancer? Why is it acceptable that a forty-five-year-old woman dies? Why is it acceptable that her back hurt and she started missing work and at Thanksgiving they said, "Maybe lupus," and two weeks later they said, "You have forty tumors on your spine, you have spots on your liver." "Spots," they always said, as if they were harmless dots or stains or the whirling glitter-dust you see when you're dizzy. She was forty years old then.

People have asked me in hushed voices whether she had children. They always ask this if they do not know, and they nod, satisfied, to hear she did not. But she wanted children, wanted them fiercely and could not conceive, and why is it better that she could not have them? Better that her wish was not granted? Better that there are no little Kathryns running around? They might have cleverly ditched out of household chores, as she did as a child, they might be physically fearless, they might play the flute and speak five languages, they might be a continuation of her here on earth.

I want to lay my hand on her head, on the pink cap. During the second summer, during a family reunion in the Dordogne, she let me soak clean cloths with heated olive oil and lay them on her back. Two or three times I did that, when her husband and mine were out late together. I want to touch her hands. I am afraid to disturb her body. With a touch, she might fall out of her fixed position. I just stand there, not touching her and not speaking. I'm not prepared. She never wanted to be thought of as terminally ill. She didn't aspire to be the dying sage, the family wise woman, and yet she became that, feeble and knowing, graceful with pain. We knew, and we also very deliberately did not know that she was dying, because together, with her will and all of ours, we held her with us among the living, who are not to be pitied, who will survive.

I leave Bad Aibling in the late afternoon, alone, to get back to my children. I ride in a white van, in the rain, winding through small towns where the shops glow with golden light—full of pastries and fresh bread and chocolate, wooden toys, and expensive shoes—to the Munich airport. The finality of leaving makes me slump against the seat. At the airport, my e-ticket works, I buy a magazine in English, and the airline dispenses free *USA Todays* in the boarding area. Once again I am in transit, and the plane lifts me out of Germany, terrible country of death. I hope never to come back. On the plane I sit next to a young Brit who thumbs through a modular shelving catalog, shopping for the perfect unit. He shares an apartment in Sophia Antipolis, the mini-Silicon Valley of the South of France, where computer executives work in office parks surrounded by golf courses. What an idiot this guy seems, as he natters about "maximizing space." It's Friday night, he's been working in Munich all week, and he hopes his roommates have stocked up on beer. He is a stolid mass of bubbling triviality, and when he asks me my business in Germany, I say only that I've been visiting family. Yet he is a relief to me, as we rise together over the dark soaked forests, lifting and turning toward the south.

Bad Aibling is in us now, the place we can't leave behind. How absurd, really, that I will always resent the cheerfulness of an oompah band in lederhosen that plays at night in a museum courtyard there. Every place in Germany exists in relation to it, the little town with too many pharmacies. This paralysis is, to me, the official flip side of the beer commercial moments Kathryn always chased—the moments when time stops in a golden intimate perfection, moments we were lucky to share with her, like drinking New Year's champagne on the roof of a Manhattan apartment building while the fireworks blossomed above, or watching her marry Tim in a dress she designed herself under the huppah in Philadelphia's oldest synagogue during the minute of the stars' most propitious alignment, or having a picnic on Hampstead Heath on a soft summer day. The flip side is that time stopped for us in Bad Aibling. A way of being stopped there, a conversation, a tension. We stretched out the string, and thumbtacked it down on Bad Aibling.

We keep moving all summer, following all of our plans as if following them will keep us in Kathryn's company. We travel to rented houses around France with Tim and assorted relatives, and we keep jumping in cars to convoy to noteworthy towns, chateaus, wineries, markets, restaurants, swimming lakes, and fêtes, moving swiftly along the country roads. Guidebooks in hand, we drive to coastal Arcachon for a shellfish lunch and sandcastle-building, zip off to the Bordeaux airport to pick up a new arrival, sidetrack to Saint-Émilion to buy tablecloths, go back to the house to whip up a fantastic curry dinner. This racing around—and the hours spent relaxing in the upholstered dining rooms and dappled terraces of Michelin-starred restaurants, eating pâté while pacifying the younger children with crayons and baguette and pasta and twirling on the lawn and standing on benches to wave at boats ruffling down the adjacent river—invokes the spirit of Kathryn.

So we keep to her plans, returning to London before we fly home to the States, until finally we arrive at the last plan, our daughter's tenth birthday at the Rainforest Café at Piccadilly Circus. That night as the neon of Piccadilly bathes us and we buzz in and out of record shops, we imagine Kathryn conceiving of the plan. At the restaurant we choose good wine for the grownups, and buy souvenirs for the kids, just as if she is with us there and we feel festive and generous. The restaurant staff has Cade stand on a chair and hold her birthday cake as they sing to her. "Maximum humiliation," she says later, but it is a Kathryn moment, the candleglow illuminating Cade's shining face.

And then we go home, all the way back to Pennsylvania. No reason to keep moving now. We had been running on last plans, on vapors. We let our son's passport expire. Our passports once seemed almost animate, glowing with readiness in my top dresser drawer. We had passports, flight passes, cash, credit cards—we could be out the door in an hour. Now in the early evening between work and dinner my husband will jump up and pace restlessly—it's the perfect time to call Kathryn in London. I will hate to say my name on the phone when I call the family because it might give them a jolt. I was always the second Kathryn, and to my nieces and nephews Aunt Kathryn Two—now I am just the wrong one. Sometimes we will come upon an object we have forgotten—a piece of silk she brought from China, a bracelet from a healing ceremony—and then it is as if she is with us still. But mostly our transit is over, and we sit in chairs as if thrown there, heavy with inertia. This is the deathplace, the place we are, where the potentialities are shutting down and we drift through the house, going nowhere, watching the dust of what was catch the light. We remember the Italian police stopping us for speeding in the Alps, and laughing at us as we tried to explain in mashed bits of French-German-English that my husband's sister had died in the night, the night before, she was dead of cancer, and we were driving straight through to Bad Aibling, we were driving fast, we were racing as fast as we could to get there.

A Gift

Oldest child gave me a white teapot embossed with fleur-de-lis, and it reminds me of the South of France, with all its ceramics and Mediterranean coastline and Napoleonic reenactors. I love the South of France. There, people live naturally in medieval stone houses flanked by vineyards and lavender. And I love the real South of France, where the pristine-ness co-exists with the Quik drive-thru burger place, shopping malls and factory brand shoe outlets—not to mention gas stations, rusty soccer stadiums, chemical-fuming hair salons, and concrete apartment blocks.

Oldest child, Cade, gave me a teapot. She is a good gift giver, being a fine knitter, baker, photographer and CD-burner. On this rainy day I love my teapot even more than tea—I love the idea of a teapot and the vision it summons of sitting in a chair reading with a cup of tea. I should really do that sometime. Today I made tea but then youngest child, Benjamin ("I'm the greatest one," he declares, "can you tell everyone that?"), got a dollar bill stuck in his dollar bill magic trick, and middle child, Jacob, needed his tie tied, and then lost a collar button five minutes before we had to leave the house. "I can't believe you know how to sew on a button," he said gratefully as I re-affixed a collar button, skillfully not stabbing him in the chest. (What has mothering come to if this ability is surprising?) He was headed off to a quiz bowl competition an hour away, and he looked ready for TV in a white shirt and skinny tie and cardigan. I tried to identify the exact moment in my children's lives when "I want my mommy" metamorphosed from the real to the ideal; i.e., from when actual mom's presence would suffice to when the kid wailed for the idea of a perfect matriarchal figure that instantly banished all pain. I think it was around age three.

Oldest child gave me a teapot, and these days I do drink tea. When I lived in the South of France during a cold winter in an unheated apartment, I drank tea to stay warm, and then I didn't want to drink it for the next two decades.

Globe

Here is a little song from Gertrude Stein:

Once upon a time the world was round and you could go on it around and around. Everywhere there was somewhere and everywhere there they were women children dogs cows wild pigs little rabbits cats lizards and animals. That is the way it was. And everybody dogs cats sheep rabbits and lizards and children all wanted to tell everybody all about it and they wanted to tell all about themselves.

That is the beginning of a children's book called *The World Is Round* that I found in a used bookstore in Hay-on-Wye, England. And it completely explains travel writing to me.

The elementary students here participate in Knowledge-a-thon, for which they memorize the answers to one hundred questions, and get orally quizzed. Geographically, this year's third-graders need to know the river that flows past Harrisburg (Susquehanna), the national park closest to our school (Gettysburg National Military Park), three countries in Asia, the longest rivers in the United States (the Missouri) and the world (the Nile), the six states that touch Pennsylvania, which European country is shaped like a boot, the seven continents of the world, and the largest freshwater lake in the world (Lake Superior). Youngest child and I review the questions at the bus stop. He wants to get one hundred percent.

Have you done your homework? I ask ever so delicately of middle child after I have fed and watered him. *Don't tell me what to do,* Jacob says. *Are we going to watch the new episode of* Psych? I ask him. *Don't tell me how to live my life,* he says. *The fan should keep you cool,* I tell him as I say goodnight. *Don't tell me what will happen,* he says.

Gertrude Stein didn't tell us what to do, how to live, or what would happen. I'll just stick with the facts: It's 25,000 miles around the earth. The moon orbits the earth in twenty-nine days. The sun sets in the West, the eyelid has the thinnest skin, and *Charlotte's Web* is fantasy fiction because Charlotte can talk and writes words in her web. We live in the twenty-first century.

Blue Coast

After my parents divorced, my sister and I didn't live with our father anymore, and for a stretch of our teenaged years, he took us on edifying trips in August. Who were we, and where did we belong in the world? Through traveling we would learn. The summer I turned sixteen, we went to France.

One night we slept at a train station. Heads on our duffel bags, we slept on benches near the tracks. When the sun rose a number of Muslim men unrolled rugs on the nearby grass and began to pray, facing their spiritual home. We were now in our spiritual home, Europe. (Defined broadly enough to include England, it was our ancestral home, too.) Inside the station, in the high-ceilinged waiting room, men in rumpled business clothes performed ablutions, slapping spicy aftershave on their necks. I remember the sound of a man singing as he slapped his neck, against the huff and release of espresso machines.

We took a walk behind the station, down to a wide canal, and imagined how we could ride a barge or live on a houseboat. I had read *Dove*, the true story of a family that sailed around the world, and asked my father if we could do that, half wishing for a reprieve from high school, half wishing to become as sinewy and worldly as the boy on the book's cover, who stood on the bow calmly gazing at Polynesia. We had the potential to be adventurers, having slept in the open air.

My father had bought us each a duffel bag before the trip, and instructed us sternly that we could bring no other luggage. I loved the feeling of having all that I needed in one bag, at hand. I looped my arms through the straps and carried it like a sausage-y backpack. We were in a small town in Provence, standing on a train platform in the morning. Headed for the coast, land of the Cannes Film Festival, and Princess Grace of Monaco. Those words *the coast* conjured up a glitter of possibility—like a film strip flicking across projection light, like tiara diamonds—of far horizon, from where we stood on the dry bank of a brown canal. Patricia Hampl called the Côte d'Azur, "The ultramarine basin of what used to be called Western Civilization." We boarded a train for the source.

That night we drove around the port of Nice. There were fishing boats all rigged up with red nets and gear, and then, anchored in deeper water, white yachts and cruise ships, their golden windows like party lights strung against the black sea. We wound up a hill above the port, steeply, to our hotel, and then explored, in the dark, the plush trimmed lawns of the fancier hotel next door. Lighted paths curved through its sloping property, where we stood on stone stairs to look down at the boats. I felt smugly adult that I could appreciate the view, could appreciate the difference between the two hotels, ours being modest but a better deal. We could sneak our way into this fancy South of France; we could stay in the cheap hotel and then sweep down into the city like anybody else.

My father drove us down the Promenade des Anglais, the route along the water built in the 1820s by English expatriates as a walkway for taking the sea air. Near the center of town a lit carousel turned and a band played in a gazebo. We followed a footpath toward the music. I wore a black gauze sundress, with straps that tied at the shoulder, and high-heeled slides bought in Paris. The slides had plastic heels, and cost only eight dollars, but I felt stylish, having pulled this ensemble out of my humble bag. I also wore my first real tan, from sunbathing devotedly using Bain de Soleil orange gelée (more sophisticated than Coppertone), burning and peeling while I read magazines. It is strange to be a teenage girl, to be looked at. When you are skinny and have clear skin and are sixteen years old, it is not delusional to imagine that boys are looking at you. They use their imaginative x-ray vision to see through your clothes, and this seemed natural, as if I had been growing up solely to arrive at this moment of being measured for the shine of my hair and eyes and teeth and lips. The small curve of my breasts. The swing of my dress. The crunch of my heels on the gravel. My every step was registered by a line of slouching boys in the park, as I moved into the halo of music and light and stood there with my father and younger sister.

We watched the crowd of people dancing to rock music, the electric guitar incongruous with the Victorian gazebo. A boy appeared. He stood in front of my father, asking permission to dance with me. How foreign his manners were—a boy at home would ask me directly. He wore a midnight blue button-down shirt, untucked, and black trousers, not jeans. My father said yes, waved him toward me, and the boy took my hand, leading me to the floor. He had a hairless chest, his shirt unbuttoned one more than the boys at home would. I smiled over at my dad and at my sister, who was thirteen and might have been wistful, or bored. After a few songs, my father took her to Festival des Glaces, reputed to offer one hundred flavors of ice cream. They would come back in an hour.

Then the boy walked me off the dance floor and picked a flower. He slid it into the teeth of my hair comb, and led me into the shadows on the lawn, beyond the spotlit palms. In the liquid green of the shadow, I felt adrenalined, not knowing what would happen, not having known this could happen, a boy seizing me from the evening's aimless family narrative of strolling the city. The boy kissed me—he pulled my hair straight down in back to lift my chin and bit my lip—and said we should go somewhere. I would have gone almost anywhere. To be chosen by a French boy was superior to being chosen by an American boy. (I had studied French in high school rather than Spanish—only years later did it occur to me that I had favored the language that seemed more upper class.) The boy spoke urgent bits of sentences in French and ran his hands over me, me wearing nothing but underwear and a dress that could float right over my head.

We crossed the Promenade, took steps down to the beach. When my plastic heels caught on the stones, he held me up. The beach had no lights. Low waves broke with a slap. A voice shouted for him, and he waved. A pack of boys came over. We need a place to go, he seemed to be saying to them, and they all talked rapidly and then he turned to me and explained that his friend had an apartment nearby. He named a street, pointed behind the park. One of his friends said in English, "You like records, yes? We have a lot of records, just come." In the dark I could see the gloss of their eyes hunting over me while the one boy kept his arm around my bare shoulders. I had an image of what it would be like, them doing it to the American girl while the record turned around and around. Turning, I moved quickly toward the steps as they shouted to me—"Please, c'mon"— and the one boy was polite enough to walk me coldly back to the edge of the park. I sat on a bench. When my sister came back, I said, "What kind of ice cream did you have?" I shut up that sequence in a cabinet in my head with all of the other sequences like that, which occur when you are a girl who is entranced with being wanted. And I chose to recollect instead my gauze dress and Parisian heels and a pink flower in my hair.

One day we drove east on the Bord de Mer, the low road bordering the sea, and then swung up onto the hilly peninsula of Cap d'Antibes, driving past walled estates with topiary shrubs. We paused respectfully at the gates to a renowned destination of the wealthy, the Hôtel du Cap-Eden-Roc. My father respected wealth, and the ingenuity it implicitly expressed. He had taken us to the mansions of Newport, and the Hearst Castle in California, directing us to appreciate properly the swimming pool laid with handpainted Italian tiles or a curving balustrade carved from a single piece of wood, or the model railroad built for the children by the man who had built the actual American railroad, Andrew Carnegie, the Scottish immigrant who created the steel industry from nothing. The rich were smarter than we were, or their ancestors had been, and we could at least show our intelligence by admiring their work.

We were supposed to be impressed, though subtly. Just the summer before, standing in the cavernous Great Hall of The Breakers, the seventy-room summer cottage of Cornelius Vanderbilt II, my father had seemed annoyed that I wasn't sufficiently awed by the features the tour guide was lavishly explaining. So I dropped my jaw. This struck me as the right way to show marvel and astonishment at the forty-five-foot ceiling, and the items actually owned by Marie Antoinette. I would please my father by showing an acute understanding of the importance of all this 1890s stuff. Cornelius Vanderbilt II had been President and Chairman of the New York Central Railroad. Did I care? I probably cared more about whether my hair scarf matched my T-shirt. My father snapped me out of my act. "Shut your mouth," he hissed, "Don't stand around gawking like that." (I'm still startled, still ashamed, when I recall it.) I was gawking, like a hick, a country bumpkin, an idiot, a farm girl from Kansas at the World's Fair, a tourist. I shut my mouth. My face grew hot, so I turned away. I was supposed to be appreciative of the houses of the rich, yet also—somehow—at home. Maybe our Colonial American lineage had cast us in the role of fallen nobility. We were supposed to follow the general principles for traveling, too. Never lose your cool. Always blend in. Act like you belong.

In France at the Eden-Roc, my father, sister and I stayed in our car. Presumably it wasn't a place one just strolled into. We noted the groomed flowerbeds and the driveway rolling beyond our reach. We imagined celebrities drinking champagne on a terrace. Then we drove to Saint-Tropez and drank Coca-Cola in a café and my father bought me a chocolate-brown T-shirt with cap sleeves that said Saint-Tropez in white Art Deco lettering. (I wore it for two summers after, feeling surely sophisticated.)

Nice was glamorous and mild, with its tropical gardens, blue sea, and old stucco buildings in softened yellows and ivories. During the day, we drove around exploring with the windows rolled down, and when the traffic jammed up, my father would tip his head out the window and yell, "*Qu'est-ce qui arrive?*" "What's going on?" He barely spoke French, though he liked trying. He had visited Cannes on shore leave. A navigator, he flew off the carrier *USS Forrestal* during 1961, recording each day's landings in a black leather flight log in impeccable capital letters. (He had worked as a draftsman over college summers, and never lost the handwriting.) On leave, he and his buddies stayed in an apartment next to a mansion, which they wandered into one evening as there seemed to be an open cocktail party going on, only to find themselves in a plushly decorated whorehouse. Thereafter, the American naval officers and the prostitutes spent their days on the beach together, the prostitutes practicing English, the naval officers ogling bare breasts. He still did that, checking out the topless beach scene as he drove. He would veer over to the shore side of the road until I yelled at him, "Hey, *qu'est-ce qui arrive?*"

We drove the high corniche to Monaco and walked the harbor, my father pointing out the equipment and appointments of the best sailboats. Trooping down rows of luxury cruisers, we were startled to see Jacques Cousteau's boat, the *Calypso*, unpretentious and workmanlike among the yachts. My sister and I had seen many episodes of *The Undersea World of Jacques Cousteau*, with the old Frenchman picking his way across a boat deck crowded with equipment, explaining what he would do, and then falling backwards into the sea in his scuba gear. Cousteau, like the founder of Club Med, occupied an ascetic niche of French culture, in which one pursued pleasure in a very specific way, involving minimal bikinis, fresh air, hard beds and communal activities. (The official purpose of Club Med, founded in 1950, was "to develop an appreciation for the outdoor life and the practice of physical education and sports.") In 1943 Cousteau had coinvented the aqualung breathing apparatus so that divers no longer had to wear heavy helmets. He could swim with a camera, giving us a dreamy, fishlike view of the sea. A millionaire had given the money to buy *Calypso*, a former minesweeper, which Cousteau outfitted with a lab and underwater television gear. Not that you'd guess its value, looking at the 400-ton beat-up boat.

We walked on, noticing the offbeat now as we crossed the parking lot, smiling at a VW camper van painted in a tie-dye pattern, petting a cat on a leash. Cousteau was the antidote to the garish casinos sitting squat and beckoning at water's edge, and to the aristocratic boutiques and mansions perched above.

We could never fit in, in France, except in a France devoted to science, and earthy satisfactions, rather than money. Even in our best dresses and sandals, my sister and I were not dressed as well as French girls were, with their hair in neat braids, their collared shirts crisp and tucked in. American preppiness had not infiltrated Europe yet, so our usual tennis shirts and shorts seemed boyish and sloppy as streetwear. I wanted to be crisp and tucked in, and had a sudden desire for outfits—the pale pink sweater to match the pale pink jeans in the window of Courrèges was irresistible—or maybe just a longing to fit in.

In fact we didn't have much money, and those outfits would never be mine. We had slept in the train station, and one night at a restaurant we couldn't cover the check. We were by the port of Nice, sitting at a sidewalk table, and when the bill was presented, my father realized he was short. Credit cards weren't used then so often; he must have needed to pay in francs. So he raised his eyebrows, stuffed his wallet back in the pocket of his khakis, and disappeared inside the restaurant. My sister and I sat hunched and worried, wondering if we would be washing dishes, or taken to the police station. Our father loved breaking the rules—in our early childhood he had been offered membership in the Cumberland Lawn Tennis Club in Hampstead, England, after posing as a competitor in the French Open—but money was money. We cautiously looked over at the lit entranceway. Our father waved us in. Come in, come in, he was waving, and then he was standing with his arm around the restaurant owner's shoulder, and we were all staring at a plaque on the wall of the back dining room. "The Cornell School of Hotel and Restaurant Management," the plaque read. Our father had earned his doctorate in philosophy at Cornell. "Isn't this amazing," he was saying, "the owner's son has just graduated from Cornell. We've been talking about Ithaca." Drawing us toward him, he said proudly, "My girls were born there."

Soon we were eating flaming ice cream crêpes, and the next day we visited the owner at his villa high above Nice. The Mediterranean lay before us in a sweep of blue.

The Hôtel du Cap-Eden-Roc, set on two dozen acres of ornamental gardens, had been built in 1863 as a mansion. A hotel as of 1870, it drew Americans after World War I, when the rich expatriates Sara and Gerald Murphy rented it for the summer, the off-season at that time. Twenty years after I'd first seen the hotel, I paused again outside its stone gates, with my two children in the back seat, my husband beside me. I didn't get out of the car this time either. I had come to see where the Riviera had been invented as a literary outpost.

F. Scott Fitzgerald cast the Hôtel du Cap as the Hôtel des Etrangers in his novel *Tender Is the Night*. As characters, Gerald and Sara became an American psychiatrist and his wife, Dick and Nicole Diver. In the novel, Dick and Nicole seem so entirely comfortable with themselves and their station in life, and maybe it is their comfort that fascinated me as I read both the biographical and fictional stories of their lives—not so much the money itself as the way they felt at home with it, their happy matter-of-factness about how to live and where they belong. On a shopping expedition, Nicole contentedly buys: "colored beads, folding beach cushions, artificial flowers, honey, a guest bed, bags, scarfs, love birds, miniatures for a doll's house . . . a dozen bathing suits, a rubber alligator, a travelling chess set of gold and ivory, big linen handkerchiefs . . . two chamois leather jackets of kingfisher blue and burning bush from Hermes . . ." In contrast to the fledgling film star who accompanies her and buys a "sensible" two dresses, two hats, and four pairs of shoes, Nicole's shopping expresses an infinity of money. "For her sake," Fitzgerald writes, "trains began their run at Chicago and traversed the round belly of the continent to California . . . and link belts grew link by link in factories . . . "

Fitzgerald didn't grow up rich. By the time he was two years old, his father's furniture factory in St. Paul, Minnesota, had failed, his father had lost a job as a wicker furniture salesman, and the family had moved to Buffalo for his father's new job as salesman for Proctor & Gamble. Fired from that job in 1908, when Fitzgerald was fourteen, he would not be successful in business again. When Fitzgerald's first novel *This Side of Paradise* sold well in 1920, he did not exactly display an ease with wealth: he used five dollar bills to light cigars, and called for hotel bellboys to bathe him.

With my husband and children, I planned to see the famous hotel, then find the beach the Murphys frequented, La Garoupe. In *Tender Is the Night*, the Hôtel des Etrangers has a small beach, from which Dick Diver carefully rakes the stones and seaweed each morning, creating an eccentric idyll by the sea. In fact, the Hôtel du Cap occupied a clifftop, and the beach lay a half mile away over the peninsula's hills. La Garoupe was an unappreciated stretch of sand in the 1920s, with forested hills rising on three sides behind it and a clear view of the sea straight ahead. The Antibes peninsula was wild and undeveloped then, traversed only by unpaved roads. The Murphys bought a house, near the remains of the medieval village of Tarm seven hundred feet over the sea, and called it Villa America. Every morning, Gerald painted in his studio on the grounds while the children had lessons, and Sara planned menus, or consulted with the gardener. Before noon the family and their guests would head down the road to the beach, where everyone sunbathed and swam. The adults sipped chilled sherry under umbrellas. After the beach, the crowd would assemble for lunch on the villa terrace, followed by a siesta, and then an expedition. The children would bathe and eat dinner while the adults dressed for the evening. Gerald would make his own invented cocktails, and a group of friends would settle in for an evening party in the garden. Sara had a shorthand for their evenings, DFG, or Dinner-Flowers-Gala.

The Murphys employed a cook, gardener, studio assistant, nanny, tutor, housekeeper, and driver. At home, in small-town Pennsylvania where my husband and I had settled in as college professors, I read "Dinner-Flowers-Gala" and laughed to think that my version of an evening was Dishes-Garbage-Laundry.

In France, as my husband, children and I pulled into the crowded La Garoupe beach parking lot, a chilled sherry sounded perfect, with the kids squirming in the back seat, disappointed at the rainy weather. I had been hoping to find Villa America with its handpainted stars-and-stripes sign, and to have a sense of the Murphys' existence, which focused on the creative pleasures of art—applied equally to doing calisthenics on the beach, making a painting, organizing a children's scavenger hunt, or hosting twelve for dinner. However easy it was to dismiss them as frivolous and rich, I admired them. It takes grace and energy to confer everyday life with a sense of ceremony.

We couldn't find the villa, among the many busy streets that now crisscross Cap d'Antibes, among the hundreds of villas behind hedges and iron gates, topped with satellite dishes. And La Garoupe beach, raked clean and reveled in during the summer of 1923? La Garoupe beach was gone, as the Murphys knew it, now crammed with private beach-restaurant concerns, with two narrow bits of public beach spliced in. Wooden decks spread out in front of the pricey uninspiring restaurants, with chaise longues and umbrellas for rent. Women emerging from the restaurants after lunch were cheaply dressed up, in gold sandals and skintight clothes. A woman in gold lamé pants carried a cake box, striking the impression that the restaurants were the type you held parties in because of the standard fancy menu and the water view.

We walked a path around the point, where waves crashed against black rocks. I could imagine how the beach would have been lovely, as I looked back from the point at the tight C-shaped cove, the beach punctuated by large rocks at either end, the hills of forest rising behind.

Having paid obeisance to the Eden-Roc, and declining to take any photos of the depressing La Garoupe beach, we drove the peninsula in what had become a downpour. We ran into a café for Oranginas and beer. I'm sure my father had a beer when he took me and my sister out for sodas; a single glass of beer has a way of smoothing out the afternoon for a traveling parent. We bought vintage postcards of the Côte d'Azur. Three women pose in different seasonal outfits on a 1936 card, advertising the coast as not just for winter visitors, but for spring, fall, and summer, too. In 1936, the year of my father's birth, the Riviera in July was still a fresh idea. Half a century or so later, fast-food restaurants and American-style malls had their place on the coast alongside the yachts and pines and castles. Jets roared low over the ugly rocky beach at Cagnes-sur-Mer, below the landing route for Nice. Our kids picked around litter, finding azure sea glass among stones and wrappers.

A writer can travel in all classes, and yet belongs in none of them, always outside or in disguise, never truly in. Fitzgerald the visitor watched Sara and Gerald Murphy crossing paths in their high garden on a summer afternoon and wrote them into characters. My husband and I finally went to the Eden-Roc for lunch. Indeed, one does not stroll into the place. A kind man in a suit interviewed us at the front door, identifying our leased car in the gravel lot, ascertaining that we had secured a reservation, looking us up and down as we squared our shoulders in our not-so-good best clothes. He swept us in with an arm, free to descend marble steps and occupy a table overlooking the water. Unattainable yachts bobbed. We drank wine and smiled at the limitless sea.

Another day my husband met friends at the Eden-Roc and sat at a table next to the singer Beyoncé. Thereafter, every time we saw her in a magazine or on television, one of us would say, *You ate lunch next to her.* He was the interloper, she the citizen of the terrace overlooking the sea. One day we visited La Garoupe beach and paid the hundred dollars for cushioned lounge chairs, flanked by umbrellas and attended to by waiters bearing trays. We swam in the murky water, and we stood, just as Gerald Murphy had, on the sand and gazed out past the cove to the sea. It was lovely, our Villa America. Later when we drove up into the hills to cook spaghetti we looked down on the nightly glitter, our view spanning from the Nice observatory to the lighthouse at La Garoupe. As writers we had the elixir: we could imagine our way into the glittering world.

At sixteen, I knew Europe as the model of civilization and myself as a privileged person because I could travel there. A sense of being at home there, begun with a kindergarten year in London, had evolved when I was ten, and my father took us all to Devon, in the west country of England, to see where his ancestors had lived. I didn't know this would be our last family trip, before he and my mother separated. I didn't know that just as my childhood home disappeared, a new sense of home would rise on the horizon.

On our grandfather clock at home, a sun and moon revolved over the face of the clock, which chimed every quarter hour. The lemon sun would fall off to the left, a silver moon rising to take its place. Devon began to rise as an idea, and the Rhetts as a family whose name transcended my lifetime, my country. We stayed in a Victorian wood-shingled inn with deep porches, and vast green lawns. My father showed me a family bible, larger than my mother's law books or the encyclopedias we had at home. I hadn't known what a family bible was. He carefully turned back the leather cover and thick ivory pages, placing his index finger here, and there, on a name.

When my father left our house, he took his clothes, the gold pocket watch under a glass dome on his dresser, and, most noticeably, the grandfather clock. Family tradition dictated that the eldest son would choose among his father's most precious possessions at the time of the father's death, my father told me that year. (As second son, my father had watched his brother Bill choose their father's valuable Vacheron minute repeater watch.) Maybe my father's departure from our household felt like a precursor to death, or his absence was a kind of death to him and to us. What would I remember him by? His two precious possessions were the gold watch and the grandfather clock. "Which would you choose?" he asked me, as I had to stand in for an eldest son. Today, more conscious of the past, I might ask for the watch, a retirement gift from the railroad for which my great-grand-father worked, having started as a track boy after running away from home. Then, I answered, "the clock," and so my father showed me how to wind it with a key when it ran down, and how to set it in motion again by pulling the pendulum to one side and letting it go. The clock was tall and imposing, as he was. He so admired the craftsmanship of it, from the delicate painting of the pale sun and moon, to the solid brass cylindrical weights, that the clock itself stood as an expression of all he thought proper and well-made in life. Most important, the clock as family heirloom stood for history, the traceable story of a family, in which I was beginning to see my place.

At sixteen, as a lodger in a château in Provence where we stayed before heading to the coast, my father, sister, and I sat arrayed on stiff chairs in a formal salon. I accepted the host's offer of a cigarette and glass of wine. My father raised his eyebrows and said nothing. What are you going to do about it, I telegraphed with a smirk. I was just attempting to belong, in one of the strange places he had dragged me to. The end of my childhood education, this would be our last father-daughters trip. Velvet drapes subdued the daylight. Several arrangements of satin-upholstered sofas and chairs gleamed, flanked by musical instruments on stands, presided over by oil por-traits framed in gilt. This way of life, gracious and cultured and softened with age, was civilized. The childhood ballet and piano lessons, the adolescent reading of European novels, was supposed to prepare me to sit easily in the satin chair. We made small talk in French with our host.

Later, outside, we whipped off our good manners like costumes to play basketball in the driveway. My father called me fat. I beat him at free throws. No idea could contain us.

Tourist

"And you will probably want to stroll about wherever you
please, pause in the shaded terrace of a café, dream in front of
paintings, enamels, sculptures, or other works of art, decoration or
collection, and have time for a shopping spree."
—Museum and Tourist Office brochure,
Saint-Paul de Vence, France

How humiliating it is to be a tourist. When my husband and I moved
to a small town in rural Pennsylvania with our two children, we
promised ourselves that we could go away every summer. We recognized that we were urbanites, Europhiles. It's too bad we realized
that only after accepting a job and buying a house. *Oh well, I'm sure
all is for the best.* In any case, we decided to travel when we could,
and one year we lived in France for six months.

My question is, if educated people generally believe that
traveling is desirable, worthwhile, and even necessary to being a
knowledgeable, sophisticated adult, then why must tourists be made
to feel so low? Maybe my husband and I *have* passed under the
plane trees, dreaming of alternative lives—in that stone farmhouse
on the facing vineyard hill, for example—but now that the tourist
brochure has instructed us to stroll and pause, dream and shop, we
feel so unoriginal.

Here in Saint-Paul de Vence, France, the garish souvenir shops,
their offerings hung above and piled on the sidewalks outside the
medieval city walls, tell us that many have been this way before. We
are, historically, so far past the possibility of discovering anything
new that our role is laughable. We are here to see what has been
seen before, seen and manufactured into items we can tuck into our
suitcases, a lavender sachet or a little doll dressed in peasant clothes.
The tourist brochure suggests we will find it enchanting to meditate

a while by the fifteenth-century ramparts. The locals suggest with their condescending looks that we will pass through but never *know* their place. While we stand ruminating by the ramparts, reading the bronze plaque about a cannon, the locals hurry by, hauling groceries, crushing cigarettes under their sharp heels, engaged in real life.

At home, my husband and I live in a tourist town ourselves. As I walk the dog or push the stroller, double-decker buses barrel by, the open upper decks crammed with tourists wearing headphones for an audio tour of the Gettysburg battlefield. They stare at me: a typical local. I glance at them: typical tourists, on the circuit. Occasionally we cross paths, as I get caught behind a horse-drawn carriage while taking my son to a tennis lesson, but mostly they inhabit the tourist end of town, flowing from motel to museum to souvenir shop to bus tour without ever touching the elements that make up our resident lives here—the grocery or shoe store, the public schools, the bar we frequent with colleagues. In St. Paul, or wherever we go, we become the lightweight tourist stream, flowing predictably along the fortification walls and shortcut alleys. While we think of ourselves as wanderers, as creative and independent for being travelers, we ought more accurately to imagine a conveyor belt and ourselves as little bottles on it, waiting to be filled up with pretty views and *bouillabaisse* and spit back home.

As my husband and I drink our coffee in St. Paul, our two children kicking a soccer ball across the boule pit, tour group #11 walks by, their guide holding up a white placard with their number as she leads them into town. They trudge in comfortable shoes, laden with fanny packs and money belts and camera bags. Their pants zip off to become shorts. The long-sleeved shirt provides a layer over the tank top. The skirt can be wrung out over a sink and hung up to dry overnight. It is probable that every member of tour group #11 has a bit of velcro on their person. We are sitting easily at the Café de la Place watching the busloads come and go, watching a pair of sunburned Brits drink rosé at ten o'clock in the morning.

We are supposedly having a more authentic experience than the package-tour visitors, renting an apartment here during a sabbatical from work, speaking the language, driving ourselves around the roundabouts. We dress normally, though not as formally as the locals in their pressed linens. We teach our children two essential concepts: when in Rome; and the ugly American. They wonder at these. When the French visit the United States, the children ask, are they the ugly French? No, it is only the Americans—and the Germans—who are thought of the world over as obnoxious and unattractive. We explain briefly about loudness, fatness, cameras, and dressing as if we had come to mow the lawn, which is how the French view the American version of casual dress.

However, our chief crime as American tourists in France is that we are not French. There is little to be done about that. At age twenty-one on our study abroad or round-the-world trip we may have tried to appear French—or Italian—by wearing black clothing, a disdainful attitude, and a Gitane. Now we are older. We refuse to feel explicitly inferior to Europeans, although subtly we emulate them. We try to feel at home here. For many of us, the multinational region of the European Economic Union once *was* our family home. Now we're returning to look, at where our ancestors lived, at where we might have lived had they chosen not to leave. We can walk the medieval streets of the country specific to our family origins and imagine our forebears walking there. No matter how many fellow tourists tramp through, the terraced, olive-treed landscape, the sunlit air and the cobblestones remain intact for us.

"The most diverse sensitive and talented people have come here to stay, or meet at the famous 'Colombe d'Or' inn. They, too, make Saint Paul a festival for the eyes, a crucible transforming feelings and perceptions into emotions that are intense and subtle."
—Museum and Tourist Office brochure,
Saint-Paul de Vence, France

We are "the eyes," presumably, rather than the ones who "make Saint Paul a festival." We may experience a constricting self-consciousness as we photograph the view, order ham sandwiches in bad French, and shop for pottery. But we will try as hard as we can to transform our uncomfortable feeling that we are a cliché. We have paid a lot of money to be here, to gaze at the Alpes-Maritimes, to note the full goldenness of the moon. The tourist program is demanding: to wonder (or even to wonder *again*— "every stay here is a rediscovery, an opportunity for renewed wonder"), to stroll, pause, please ourselves, dream, and spend more money, fully believing that our Provençal tablecloth, when we shake it out over our table at home, will produce a special feeling. We will try to complete the program, feasting our eyes on the anguished, chainsmoking *artistes* (who reportedly are sellouts, making flowery oil paintings for us). The *artistes* are playing their roles, staying in character with their intense glances, their subtle flicks of ash. Dogs nap under the shade of trees. Newlyweds drive off in an ivy-bedecked convertible. We will dream, and drink the local wine.

Actually, my husband and I love tourist towns. We love the unspoiled hopefulness of the tourist (sightseeing has been recorded as early as 1500 B.C., by visitors to the Sphinx), striding uphill with a silvery videocam poised over one eye. We have visited tourist destinations on four continents. We have been tourists since childhood, when we poured ketchup on our omelettes in Paris. The Heisenberg Uncertainty Principle is embedded in our synapses: the observer alters what is observed. A place is deemed "real" if it remains untouristed. But we cannot visit these "real" places, for as soon as we arrive to look, the place becomes unreal, ruined, contrived. We ruin places. The local economy begins to answer our anticipated desires, the shopkeepers pandering with pottery cats and postcards and souvenir pencils; with disposable cameras, suntan lotion, maps. Even in our own estimation, we render places artificial by our very presence. Yet we love being in the company of fellow questers, meeting at must-see crossroads.

And we love the efficient passion of the tourist. We have taken ourselves out of everyday life, in which we wake and pour the cereal and blow-dry our hair and walk the dog and get to work. Now we want to see and absorb, quickly, so that we may see more. Of course there's an element of desperation. In the vernacular of Kerouac, we are "looking for it"—will we get it by sitting in the café "soaking it up" or by scrambling to every museum and shrine, or by an alchemical blending and balancing? Will we feel *it* before we have to go home? Will we, in the lingo of teens, *nail it*? We are trying to live in the present, be in the moment, but the past and future crowd in like bookends. "We're here!" we crow to each other, *here* instead of at our homely kitchen table reading guidebooks (how nice that tablecloth will look!). We reconstruct the narratives of what brought us here; and we're already forecasting the next trip, the way we sensuously plan dinner while we're still eating lunch.

We are playing *pétanque* gracelessly, we are drinking Martell, we are swimming in the cold river, we are puffing up the mountain path, we are admiring the moored yachts, we are eating croissants and panini and lamb chops, we are caught in traffic, we are straddling the cannon to be photographed, we are standing on the ramparts, we are making out despite the jet lag, we are gathering the sand toys, we are explaining the release of prisoners in Paris that is the *raison d'être* for these fireworks, we are connecting Bastille Day to our Fourth of July, the day we were no longer a colony of Great Britain, under the general rubric of freedom from tyranny. We are humbled, tasteless, defiant. We are the former colonists, prisoners, and peasants. Not to worry—we're just back for a visit.

The Lonely Wanderer

"Guys disappear in Asia." This is a sentence Diana Elliott of the State Department's Philippines Desk of the Citizens Emergency Center offered on the telephone.

It is a kind of death sentence I first heard in 1990 in northern Thailand about a traveler or expatriate or exile, take your pick, who had failed to return from a motorcycle trip to the region where Thailand, Laos, and Burma converge and form what is known as the Golden Triangle, a center of opium trafficking in Southeast Asia. Guys disappear in Asia. Which means, specifically, that white American men for one reason or another abandon all connection to family and home and country. Or they get killed. For one reason or another.

For what reason, Diana Elliott wanted to know, was this person in the Philippines?

The only employment I knew Bruce Oliver had for sure was buying and distributing cocaine for a brief period in Dare County, North Carolina. This was verifiable because he was arrested, along with his girlfriend.

According to the trial record, the "Defendant met co-defendant in January or February 1983 when he entered the County to sell some of his property there." Supposedly "in the area on business," Bruce had been staying "in the guest room" of the woman identified at trial as "co-defendant"—but known within the family, that is to say outside of the judicial process, as "his girlfriend"—for three months when police officers, having obtained a warrant, "entered the home" at 2:15 in the morning. Upon entering, they were rewarded with the sight of Bruce Oliver running down the hallway with a plate of cocaine in his hand. Waiter-style, I imagine, with his long brown hair streaming behind him. "Defendant threw the plate in the air, it landed on a bed, and a white powdery substance—later identified as cocaine—fell on the bed." The officers then found a dream inventory of evidence: a set of Ohaus Triple Beam Scales, a weighing plate, two small measuring cups, a sifter, a plastic straw, a razor blade, business records, and, of course, numerous Baggies of cocaine.

None of the seized items belonged to Bruce Oliver, although his fingerprints turned up on the plate, the scales, and both an outside corner and an inside corner of a plastic bag. In the defendant's defense, he was "surprised and shocked at the presence of drugs and drug paraphernalia at [the] co-defendant's home." He had not seen any of these items prior to being awakened in the middle of the night of the arrest, at which point, "out of curiosity he examined some of the items in the home, but did not bag, package, or repackage any of the substances." No drugs were found on his person, or in his clothing, or in his car. Bruce Oliver testified that "he does not use drugs." Bruce Oliver testified that, at the moment when officers "entered the home," the co-defendant was "picking things up off the counter and she went down the hallway and I was sitting there watching TV. I'm a guest in her home and at that point I had stood up and there were two plates on the end of the counter, and I picked them up and I walked down the hallway."

The girlfriend's story happened to conflict with this version of events. And it is difficult to piece together a convincing narrative of the defendant waking up around 2:00 a.m. on an April morning, for no particular reason, watching television, happening to notice for the first time the presence of drugs and drug paraphernalia, and then picking up the scales and Baggies to examine them as if he had never seen such things before. It is difficult to imagine where he was headed with that plate. The bathroom? The officers do not mention in the trial transcript what it was exactly that caused Bruce Oliver to toss "the plate in the air."

The court sentenced Bruce Oliver to two years for possession of cocaine and to three years for possession with intent to manufacture, sell, and deliver the same cocaine. *He should have hired a better lawyer*, was a judgment heard frequently in 1983.

When he earned work release status, his brother arranged a job for him on the coast. His second job, officially.

His second job was cleaning the rental units behind his brother's fishing pier. He was thirty years old then, halfway out of prison. He complained about his teeth, which were rotting visibly, giving his smile a cringing quality, the face crumbling in on itself, an expression of failure. He needed good teeth to perform effectively as the front man for any number of operations going down in Atlanta, Miami, Bogota, and even, apparently, the less prominent locale of Dare County. Or, as he put it, he needed his teeth fixed so he could get a job.

All of which does and does not explain Manila.

That is, how it is that a person comes to be "last seen twenty kilometers outside of Manila."

Bruce always ran out of money. Always, since becoming an adult, he spent more than he earned. *Why doesn't he just get a job*, my mother asked in exasperation. He could work at McDonald's, or be a bus driver. He could do *something*. He hadn't graduated from high school. He wouldn't apply for jobs that demeaned his status, or rather, his family's status, which he conferred upon himself. He wouldn't be selling goddamned french fries for minimum wage.

During his teenage years, his father drove a black Cadillac equipped with a telephone and with a TV set for the back seat passengers, luxury features in the 1960s. The family lived in a three-story house on Porter Street in northwest Washington, D.C., in which a stained glass window hung at the landing of the grand front stairway. The back stairs were used by the children and by Mildred, the full-time nanny, cook, and housekeeper.

It should be said that Mildred was desperately needed because her mistress, Mary Louise McClellan Oliver of Fort Worth, Texas, was a hopeless alcoholic. She had no hope of returning to a sane or sober reality. At a certain point in the middle of her life, she could still wear Chanel-style suits and paint on a rosebud of lipstick and brush her wig. She could still take an interest in the activities of her toy poodles Ginger and Tammy. And she was long gone by then; though where Mary Louise ever was is actually a good question. It should be said that when Mary Louise was pregnant with her fourth child she was drunk most of the time.

Bruce was the "cool" uncle, never cooler than at his mother's post-funeral gathering, where Mildred fussed over the buffet and the politicoes talked seriously, standing up and holding cocktails. The pack of teenaged grandchildren found Bruce upstairs. Alone but not lonely, he was swigging beer from a bottle and listening to tunes, while revolving slowly in a black leather swivel chair. He wore a Hawaiian shirt under his suit coat. He was twenty-six. He smiled a welcoming and crooked smile. *Hey y'all*, he said. *You found me.* Then he closed his eyes, to better appreciate the sound. He was in the music business. I didn't know if he was sorry his mother had died.

Mary Louise had grown up being dressed by maids. When she was ten, she would stand and wait for someone to tie her hat. At the time of her marriage she did not know how to cook, having never been allowed in the kitchen. At the time of her marriage she may not have wanted to be married, but no one asked. Robert Oliver was in love with Mary Louise's older sister Laura, but he took seventeen-year-old Mary Louise to a dance one night and kept her out late. That's the nutshell sentence. If you opened up a walnut and stuffed that sentence inside, you would have the seed of everything to come. The twenty-five-year-old Robert was forced to marry her for keeping her out past curfew in Texas in 1935. She had no business being married to a union organizer for oil workers who kept getting thrown in jail. She was one of those women who looks good in photographs because life is stilled for that moment. Her small willowy body, her tilted oval face. She couldn't cook or clean or take care of two babies born within two years; the second baby was sent away for a time.

I knew Mary Louise as the decrepit mother of four, grandmother of five. In the kitchen of the family beach house, we ate at the red counter on high stools. Mary Louise could be coaxed to come perch on a high stool, at the end by the wall. She could be coaxed to flake apart her dinner with a fork. She was a cat, a mouse, a bird—a diminutive invalid creature. Mostly she consumed chocolate-covered pecans, which came in pink boxes, stacked five high in a cabinet. She consumed some variety of white liquor with ice cubes, packs of cigarettes, hours of television. She weighed less than one hundred pounds. She sat in a chair pointed at the television. She wore a silky bathrobe. She leaned forward to let us hug her when we arrived and left. She never, in our presence, opened the sliding glass doors and crossed the deck and walked down onto the sand and put her bare feet in the water. The fact that she died at age sixty-three seemed to elicit a collective pity, a sense that perhaps an early death was a blessing.

Bruce in his Hawaiian shirt at the post-funeral gathering did not seem upset that she'd died, although what Bruce seemed to be did not necessarily correspond to any knowable fact. Nineteen years later, Bruce seemed to be flying to Manila at the behest of business partners to engage in essential unspecified business that had always been called *music,* which had in effect become the code word for *drugs,* so that we in the family tried diligently to believe in the reality of a string of pop concerts being booked in Colombia or Miami.

Bruce wanted to be in the music business. He wanted it to be true on the Christmas Eve of 1989 that he and José Feliciano were working together on a song about the tragedy of Tiananmen Square, the lyrics of which went "Tiananmen, Tiananmen / So many women and men / in Tiananmen." He played the studio tape for us, José was singing, it was going to be major. My sister and I were rolling our eyes in the kitchen as we refilled the cheese plate. Was that actually José Feliciano's voice?

In the spring of 1999, a woman called my mother from Manila. She was "a friend of Bruce's," she said, and she hadn't seen or heard from him in several days, which worried her because Bruce had "no access to his wallet or passport," which had been confiscated by the Manila Hilton for nonpayment. Had he contacted any relatives in the United States, she wanted to know. Because he usually called. He usually called when he was right on the edge of a big deal. And he needed a little help to get things moving. He needed a little help to facilitate the distribution of the brilliant political ballad that would take his good friend José and himself over the top.

Diana Elliott of the State Department said reassuringly that the name Bruce Oliver did not "ring a bell" and she would have heard if he were dead. That is, if he had died in circumstances in which he could be identified, circumstances that seemed unlikely for a person who had no access to money or passport, a person involved in drug trafficking last seen standing by the side of the road twenty clicks out of Manila. In the nicest possible circumstances, an American body would be disposed of properly, via the American Embassy. These circumstances, apparently, were more probable than one might think. "People aren't shy about saying, 'This isn't my family,'" Diana Elliott commented. "They don't want to pay for the burial." The fact that she hadn't heard his name created the interesting possibility that Bruce Oliver might be alive.

Live Americans who disappear can, presumably, be found. Often in jail, which would not be an improbable location. In the jails the Americans sit and wait for American tourists to visit. The guide-books beseech American tourists to visit them and this beseechment also serves as a deterrent to drug use. The *Lonely Planet* guidebook for Thailand, for example, describes Chiang Mai prison, in Thailand's second largest city, as holding dozens of *farangs* (foreigners) on drug charges. Which didn't stop me and my husband from smoking pot in Chiang Mai—we just became so paranoid when we were stoned that we flushed the whole stash down the gleaming American-style toilet in our rented home. We were the only *farangs* on the dirt lane of pristine new row homes, and we could imagine the Thai police in their dark caps and crisp white shirts rapping on the door. We'd seen *Midnight Express*. Then our friend Art visited and we had to confess that we'd thrown away the stuff.

"That whole bag I gave you?" Art hadn't disappeared in Asia—he still wrote to his mother in Michigan—but he'd been out ten years. He lived with a woman named Aoi and her children, as well as with a number of caged birds and their pet loris who enjoyed sitting on people's shoulders. Art and Aoi lived in a large wooden house on a canal outside of Chiang Mai, and Art taught English at Chiang Mai University and at the former United States Information Agency. When he wasn't working, Art got stoned, and he was forever pulling up on his motorcycle at a prearranged spot, to show us a Buddhist temple or royal rose garden, and lighting up a joint. He had a good life. There are any number of legal and pleasant long-term situations for American guys in Asia.

Art and Aoi's bedroom was lined with books in English, set on the floor around the entire perimeter. They belonged to a friend who had left to check out the northern hills, not on a chaperoned "hill tribe trek," the touristy forays into villages of picturesquely costumed people living near the borders of Burma and Laos, but on a solo motorcycle tour, three years before. He hadn't returned. Art shrugged. "Guys disappear."

Disappearing could be said to be an extension of the American expatriate's exile. The expat leaves the home country and is said to be "out." "We've been out twenty years," Bob and Doris Rostas said to me and my husband in their apartment in Oaxaca, Mexico. Presumably a person who is "out" can come back "in," but return becomes increasingly unlikely as the years stack up. Finances are more difficult in the United States. The money from a pension or estate lasts much longer in a less expensive country. Retirees who cannot afford Arizona, for example, end up in Mexico. A life without certain amenities is experienced as depressing poverty in the States, yet has an exotic charm elsewhere. It is pleasant to wash one's clothes in a sink and hang them on a clothesline on the roof of an apartment building in Mexico, or any other reasonably hospitable cheap country. There is no need to buy new clothes for the sake of fashion, and mending, even when the repairs are visible, is acceptable. Making do is an art. Tramping all over town to procure the cheapest mangoes or pottery dishes is a worthwhile expedition. Buying food from the street carts may not be what the guidebooks advise, but one is no longer a tourist. The street food is good. An air-conditioned hotel restaurant is where the Thai prince takes tea with his entourage. Real life happens outside. A routine develops, involving a circuit of take-out stands, markets, bars, and routes home. I could imagine my Uncle Bruce on the circuit in Southeast Asia. I could imagine myself in eventual exile. The bars show American movies. The way home is on a bench in the back of a pickup truck. Green lizards flow around the walls and ceilings. One falls asleep, now that the air has cooled.

The Lonely Wanderer is a piece of music I listened to while in labor with my older son. A piano piece by Grieg, it is soothing and melodic. In the deluxe birthing room at the Carolinas Medical Center, we watched an ice hockey game without sound and listened to the collection of nineteenth-century piano music by Schumann, Chopin, and Grieg, collected under Grieg's title by a studio in West Germany. The hockey skaters appeared beautiful—gliding and crashing. The piano music took me walking through imagined hills. Tenuous. Lonely. Contractions resemble hills on the monitor graph, and they can feel like hills, or waves. The notes of music strung out along an invisible path, into nothingness, and I followed them. Each struck key a step. I was in pain. In my mind, the forest was very green.

"Everything is green," a woman says to a man in a David Foster Wallace short story. "Look how green it all is, Mitch." They are looking out of the window of a trailer home into a trash-filled yard. Either the grass visible beyond the beer cans and gravel is green, or the yard is a junk heap, depending. Depending on how you look at it. Is it very green twenty kilometers outside of Manila? Is it very green where you are standing, between the road and someone's yard on the strip of dirt shoulder, as your girlfriend glides by you in a car? The palm trees no longer seem exotic. Someone might shoot you right there, because you cannot produce the requisite amount of American dollars, or cocaine, or methaqualone, also known as Quaaludes, increasingly trafficked through the Philippines in the 1990s. Your eyes might register the tropical foliage as you fall, a final screen across your vision. Your fallen body might encroach on the property of a homeowner, who reportedly would not be "shy" about calling the American consular offices to say, "This is not my family." Or, the shooter might transport you to a secondary location where you could be killed less glaringly, falling into a heap of garbage rather than onto somebody's valuable lawn.

This is how I imagine you, standing on that last note of lonely music, rooted to the spot where the woman calling frantically on her cell phone said she saw you last.

Your last known address was what the State Department wanted to know. Would that be the Manila Hilton, or your previous address, the two-toned green Cadillac your father willed to you, in which you slept, parked on the quieter streets of Los Angeles and Las Vegas?

I had two children, a husband, a job, two cats, and a house to take care of. I couldn't just get on a plane to Manila. I got online.

There are approximately twenty-five thousand addresses in cyberspace devoted to the cause of finding people. Searching on the Lycos network for websites pertaining to "missing people" yields not only pages of websites but a list of related headings. "People who did this search also searched for," the screen reads, above the following list: Find Missing Family Members, Find by SSN Search, Finding Missing People, Find Parents, Adoption Searches, Locate Lost People, Find People Hiding, and Find People Who Do Not Want to Be Found. The mood around the various websites varies. "Find Old High School Classmates," one yellow bar blinks cheerfully. The Classmates.com website claims to have 5.3 million registered high school alumni who have added their names to a database dedicated to helping old friends connect. This is the sort of search that leads to the "Real-Life Reunions" that Classmates.com features, the sort of search that induces a person to "Send Gifts" or "Send Flowers," as the alternating icons beckoned adjacent to the eighty-six Bruce Olivers in the United States whose names and addresses appeared on the screen after a Lycos People Search. Should I pursue the Bruce Oliver of Springfield, Missouri, or the Bruce Oliver of Sneads Ferry, North Carolina? Should I "Send Gifts" or should I "Send Flowers?"

Several choices follow each name and address, the bright comradely road of "Find Old High School Friends" and the darker road of "Search Public Records." Clicking on the public records line leads to USSearch.com, the self-titled "Worldwide Leader in Public Record Information." Here, I was immediately invited to enter an approximate age ("if known") for the particular Bruce Oliver I had selected (from Raleigh, North Carolina) or to "Conduct a Search on Someone Else!" The very small word "on" indicates the less than friendly purpose of such searches, which often represent not a wishful search *for* a person, but an assault on the castle of an individual's privacy. The $19.95 Deluxe Search promised ten years' worth of home addresses and telephone numbers, as well as the names of family members, roommates, and even neighbors. This paled next to the Super Search, whereby for $39.95 one could receive in addition information about civil judgments, bankruptcies, assets, professional licenses, property ownership, and UCC lien filings. But for only an extra eight dollars, why not also search the databases for, among others, active U.S. military personnel, boat registrations, FAA pilot licenses, federal firearms and explosive licenses, and national DEA-controlled substance licenses? Why not?

Well, for one thing, at SpyHeadquarters.com I could supposedly, for $29.95, download software that would enable me to search all of those databases myself. And if the employees of SpyHeadquarters. com could access such information, then why should I pay any money at all for it? At Peoplesite.com, I could post a message with a query about Bruce Oliver in the category of "Missing Person," where 519 people had already posted such messages, for free. This method of pursuit also seemed less treacherous, more akin to helping old friends connect.

The Peoplesite.com's query board's 519 entries in the category of missing persons presented an array of losses, and of barely veiled intentions. The entry for Daniel O'Neil, for example, begins, "His son has not seen him since he was eighteen months old, now he's fourteen," and continues with, "He owes back child support," and then progresses to the rather unconvincing, "Main reason is because son would like to see him." Some entries are direct: "Operates a residential painting business in Matthews, NC . . . took a substantial amount of money." Others seem magnanimous but suspicious: "looking for this person as hier [sic] to an estate"; or, "he is due a federal refund and i am trying to find him to give it to him." Most imply domestic tragedy. "Looking for my sixteen-year-old daughter, whom I believe to be with her boyfriend Jeff Threlkeld. We need to find her because she is a cancer survivor." Or, "She is my wife and my kids have put here [sic] somewhere and they wont tell me." There are birth parents seeking children who were adopted: "Lost son—born 25 Dec 1965 at Regional Memorial Hospital, Brunswick, Maine. I'm your birth mother." There are mysterious disappearances. "Joel was last seen at Walmart in Redlands, CA around 1:00 p.m. He drives a 1995 Green Ford Mustang. Has not contacted family or friends." Or, "Cayce has a post-traumatic head injury. May have connected with an occult group or someone able to take advantage of his mental disability." And then, as candidates for that subset the Lycos Network has labeled "People Who Do Not Want to Be Found," there are people such as William Harvey "Butch" LaDoucer, who "is wanted for attempted murder. Any information you may have can be forwarded directly to FBI Special Agent Paul McCabe of the Minnesota office of the FBI." There is also a notice that "Dr.

Robert E. Kelly is WANTED by the Maine Deaf Community for sexual abuse at Governor Baxter School for the Deaf between the 50's and 80's."

I spend a lot of time at genealogy websites, where countless families are experiencing the benign triumphs of totting up another name, entering another date, finding another person who would love to attend a family reunion. And so I felt a sense of creepiness around the online search services. At PeopleSite.com, Joel in his green Ford Mustang may have deserted his family after experiencing an epiphany in the Redlands, California Walmart. Cayce, who wears glasses and carries a green nylon backpack, may have been kidnapped. And a particular Thomas Patrick Cathcart had allegedly absconded with his daughter, leaving no forwarding address for her mother. I composed my own cryptic entry for the bulletin board: "The family of Bruce Lee Oliver is searching for him. Last contact: a woman called from Manila." My message seemed as implausible and strange as any other posting. The wife of Aaron L. Reed wrote: "Went AWOL 2 yrs. ago from Okinawa, Japan, USMC. Need to find him to obtain a divorce."

Bruce Lee Oliver was not needed for anything. He was not a husband. He was not a father. He was no longer a son. And he had recently worn out the patience of his sister and brothers. It is possible that his father had collapsed on a brick sidewalk in Washington, D.C., because he was no longer taking his heart medication. The reason he was no longer taking his heart medication was that he couldn't afford it. And the reason he couldn't afford it was Bruce.

Bruce had lived with his father at times, at a beach house in Southern Shores, North Carolina. Robert Oliver lived there after retiring, with his English setter Winston. He suffered from shingles, and did not like the mind alteration caused by painkillers, so he often grimaced involuntarily from a sudden stab. He did not write his autobiography about his thirty years in the labor movement and his work as economic and labor adviser to the Marshall Plan, though he kept a large incongruous desk stuffed with his old office papers out on the sun porch. The desk, from his Washington, D.C. public relations and lobbying firm, faced a wicker seating arrangement. Robert Oliver had grown up in Corpus Christi. He cooked Tex-Mex and he cooked Southern. He made enchiladas, and ham biscuits, and two-layer chocolate cake. He did beer-batter fish in the deep fryer, turning the pieces with long tongs. He could be counted on to say, when visiting and cooking in one of our kitchens, "You haven't got a pair of proper tongs." He made shrimp cocktail. We grandchildren shelled bagsful of cold shrimp before he boiled them. At the beach house in Southern Shores, he provided a reassuringly predictable milieu from 1961 until his death in 1995.

When Bruce lived there, we didn't visit. "Lived" implies permanence; it is more accurate to say that Bruce stayed there, or passed through, his father's house a station on an indeterminate circuit of stations. Bruce was Robert Oliver's last child. Sometimes the last grandchild, Bob, stayed at the house, too, and so an odd trio of lone men occupied the odd-looking aluminum-sided ranch house that faced the Atlantic. Bob was a construction worker and would become a local radio show host. He would become a surfer. He would stop smoking pot and drinking alcohol and while in the coming years he often worked as a bartender, he remained entirely sober. He moved to Hawaii for a while and ran a juice bar. He did not seem to grow up in certain traditional ways for the family's socioeconomic class, such as attending college and getting married, but neither could his life be considered problematic.

Bruce stayed at the beach house and did not work. He slept late and made plans. The last plan—the last plan anyone in the family knew about—was the office space leasing plan for the 1996 Atlanta Summer Olympic Games. While the dimensions and content of the plan never became entirely clear, the two keywords were *space* and *Atlanta*. Space in Atlanta would be at a premium during the Games, and Bruce would be the broker for this one-time-only profit-yielding venture which required telephone calls and frequent on-site appearances. The two reasons the family knew about the Atlanta space leasing plan were that Robert Oliver talked about it, pleased to be able to assure us of Bruce's industriousness, and that Robert Oliver called all of his old friends to ask for money. He may have called it *calling in favors*. He may have decided that the space leasing plan had merit. He may have been pleased to be working the phones again, recalling the years at Robert Oliver & Associates, with the monolithic furniture and the loyal secretary Nadine and the account at the Democratic hangout on Capitol Hill, the Monocle. He may have enjoyed simply talking to business people, after years of living year-round in the seasonal community of Southern Shores, an incorporated area of pale concrete beach roads with its own fire station and sanitation facility. In his daily life he would have conversed with a neighbor, or a supermarket checker, or his son Garry who ran a fishing business, or a collection of visiting relatives, all of whom constituted a rather narrow audience for his ideas about the egregious mistake of airline deregulation, or the progress of the presidential campaign. Now he was on the telephone.

The fact that Robert Oliver was telephoning old friends, cronies and political contacts for Bruce's cause represented an alarming escalation in his generosity. Maybe he had lost his judgment. Perhaps a man in his eighties no longer cares about a professional reputation. Perhaps at that age Robert Oliver's concerns had changed. Now he devoted himself to his last, lost son who at the age of forty-one might yet turn out all right.

Maybe Bruce would turn out to be an instinctive entrepreneur. After years in the music business, supposedly booking acts for blues clubs in D.C. and working in the studio and flying in and out of cities all over the South, not to mention South America, maybe Bruce knew enough to have spied a viable opportunity. To have had an original, practical idea. In fact, he may have been on his way to becoming a self-made man, and why not provide assistance when assistance was needed? Bruce had had a terrible childhood, with Mary Louise an alcoholic and himself absorbed in work; Bruce had suffered from lack of attention and support. And Robert Oliver believed in support, especially for sons, though he had come to understand that he should have supported his daughter as well. Should have, perhaps, sent his eldest child to law school as she'd wanted instead of setting her up with a secretarial job with Lyndon Johnson when Johnson was Majority Leader of the Senate. He'd put his second child through law school. He'd bankrolled his third child's fishing business, in the beginning. Now the fishing business provided him with cash when he needed it. He could give cash to Bruce. Which he did, relying increasingly on the accounts of the fishing business, which consisted of a fishing pier, and its adjacent rental cottages, which Bruce had cleaned as a work release prisoner, and a bait and tackle shop. The fishing business incurred the kinds of unpredictable costs associated with hurricanes and rainy weather in tourist season that make even successful endeavors uncertain. Yet because Robert Oliver retained a controlling interest in the business, he was able to draw from its accounts, so that his initial investment yielded a kind of pension, a pension flexible enough to support himself. And Bruce. In 1994, Robert Oliver's daughter sent him money for a new roof for the beach house. She hesitated, I know, but concluded that she need not pay the roofing contractor directly. My mother sent a check for five thousand dollars. Which was a mistake. With Bruce traveling back and forth from Atlanta and paying rental deposits and staying in hotels, the money dwindled away.

The next year, when the beach house needed a new refrigerator, my mother didn't send money. She sent a refrigerator.

It's a nice refrigerator, *top of the line* as my grandfather would say, with crushed ice and water dispensers in the vertical double doors. It keeps the white wine crisply cold when we visit on the Fourth of July. My mother owns the house now, after an estate battle led to foreclosure. She bid for it on the steps of the Dare County Courthouse in Manteo. (Which sounds pleasingly dramatic, but as she recounts with a smile, it was not a grand courthouse; there were only two steps.)

Robert Oliver collapsed on a brick sidewalk in Washington, D.C., on a warm June day in 1995. On his way into a friend's house, where he would stay the weekend for a party, he carried a suitcase and, over his shoulder, a seersucker suit. He dressed well, his white hair combed back, a handkerchief folded in his pocket. When he collapsed he hit the back of his head, causing a hematoma which required surgery that night. The operation went well, the neurosurgeon assured my mother. But hours later the eighty-six-year-old patient suffered a massive heart attack as he emerged from anesthesia.

Bruce inherited his father's car. He inherited one-third of the beach house, which he chose to take in cash. He inherited miscellaneous furniture, including several ugly lamps, which my mother stored in the beach house garage. Not too long after the call from Manila, my mother threw those lamps away. I guess the unspoken presumption was that Bruce was either dead, or too far gone to be setting up house. When she threw away the lamps, my sister and I understood that no one in the family would call the Manila Hilton, or the State Department; that no one would file a missing person report; that nobody closely related to Bruce actually cared enough whether he was dead or alive to track him down. *What if I flew to Manila and found him*, my mother said, *and brought him back here—then what?*

When my daughter was eight she said to me, "It's interesting to have a person in your family who is gone."

"Gone?" I said distractedly. She was eating her dinner so slowly that her father and brother had left the table.

"Gone. Not dead," she said, chewing a bite of baked potato. "Like your Uncle Bruce. Nobody knows where he is, right?"

"Right," I said. "Is that interesting?"

"It's exotic," she concluded.

Exotic, from the Greek *exo*, means outside. Asia is outside of our familiarity, and Bruce is outside of our family. To think that he should be found, that he should look up and drawl, *Y'all found me*, is to presume that he should want to be inside, or that he has fallen and we could save him, or that everyone, ultimately, should be restored to their family.

"Guys lose track of their time, of their lives," Diana Elliott said with a knowing finality. Why should anyone exert themselves over a middle-aged man who didn't seem particularly interested in staying in touch, who had no known legal employment or family responsibilities, and who had never set foot in the consular section of the Embassy of the United States in Manila. He might have cast an absentee ballot there, or received a list of recommended physicians. He might have obtained a new passport, or asked for assistance in getting money, or legal representation in the case of arrest. But in no way had Bruce Lee Oliver entered into the official record.

The words "Manila Hilton" practically rhyme. If someone said "Manila Sheraton" to you, or "Manila Holiday Inn," would you remember that as "Manila Hilton?" The woman calling my mother on the cell phone said that Bruce's passport and money had been seized for nonpayment by the Manila Hilton. And so the hotel seemed a logical place to begin the search for the forty-seven-year-old probable international drug dealer Bruce Oliver. But there was an obstacle to picking up the telephone and asking a front desk clerk to check the hotel's locked-up cache of passports. There was no Hilton in Manila.

Subaru

I left my car at the mechanic's once, and when I picked it up, the keytag read: Ruby Subaru. Although I've never named a vehicle, this name came to it from elsewhere, and stuck. Ruby Subaru.

She used to belong to my-stepmother-the-pilot, and so she was in perfect shape when I bought her. The car is a 1996 model, though, and I'm no pilot, caretaker of complicated machinery, so now she's semi-trashed. I lost a piece to the sound system (a multi-CD-loader located under the passenger seat, to give you an idea of what a 777 captain considers normal), the radio knob broke, the upholstery is stained, and the drink holder is stuck shut. On the outside, she's been bashed a few times while parked, and no one left their insurance information. She gets me everywhere.

I talk to her and tell her she's a good car, especially for starting on cold mornings, her bête noire. I did a lot of begging/bargaining/praising in the waning days of her last battery. Now she's more reliable. I'm only confessing that I talk to her because David Abram said that was okay in his book *Becoming Animal*:

> *While persons brought up within literate culture often speak about the natural world, indigenous, oral peoples sometimes speak directly to the world, acknowledging certain animals, plants, and even landforms as expressive subjects with whom they might find themselves in conversation.*

Maybe Abram wasn't talking about cars or any kind of machines, but if it's okay to talk to cats and rosebushes, then why not. My cat Mel is surely a person trapped in a cat's body, and I know when the spell is broken she will thank me for not talking down to her. Abram says that "the power of language remains, first and foremost, a way of singing oneself into contact with others and with the cosmos—a way of bridging the silence between oneself and another person, or a startled black bear, or the crescent moon soaring like a billowed sail above the roof." Which settles it: if he can talk to the moon, then I can talk to my car.

The poet Keetje Kuipers even included a Subaru in her poem, "Fourth of July," which begins:

> *If I have any romantic notions left,*
> *please let me abandon them here*
> *on the dashboard of your Subaru*
> *beside this container of gas station*
> *potato salad and bottle of sunscreen.*

My Subaru has recently become expressive, with stickers and mottos. This may relate to the blogging culture: expression is just busting out all over. Wesleyan Parent. Find a cure before MS gets on my last nerve (oldest child's last nerve, more accurately, and I want to Sharpie in "daughter's" just to make things clear, but then I wonder if that's because I don't wish to be perceived as having multiple sclerosis myself, so I leave it as is). Wag more, bark less. Fight Like a Girl: MS Awareness. It's all so obnoxious, like the middle school honor roll bumper stickers (guilty) and little stick figures that advertise the gender and number of your progeny plus pets (innocent). I do love reading other peoples' stickers—unless they tell me to come to Jesus—so now I've joined their crowd. I'm readable.

Becoming readable via bumper stickers may have to do with making the invisible visible: my daughter has MS, and when she's home from college people tell her she looks "so well!", and yet inside she is not well. There is no cure for multiple sclerosis, a disease that attacks the nerves of the brain and spine. Inside she has lesions in her brain and on her spinal cord that cause pain, weakness, vertigo, vomiting, and migraine. She has lost her vision temporarily; her face, hands and feet have become numb. Inside an unpredictable devastation is taking place. Or maybe my car wears bumper stickers because eldest child has joined the minority community of 400,000 people in the United States with MS, compared to, for example, an estimated 26.5 million with heart disease; it's exciting when a celebrity gets diagnosed with MS and makes the cover of *People* magazine, so that more people will understand what it is. Or maybe it's that I'm so pissed off at her university, whose response to her probable diagnosis in her freshman year was to hand us a withdrawal slip. (She'll be a senior this year.) Their callousness made me feisty and public in a way that I would not ordinarily be. Also, the car and I are sort of old by now and care less how we appear.

How did a Subaru come to be a Subaru, you might wonder. (Or not. My students call essays "relatable" or "not relatable" so often that I've started to use the word to make myself comprehensible to them. Is musing about Subaru a relatable question?) Charmingly, the first president of Fuji Heavy Industries, Kenji Kita, believed that Japanese cars should have Japanese names, and when no one in the company came up with an appealing name for their first passenger car, in 1954, Mr. Kita "gave the car a beautiful Japanese name that he had been quietly cherishing in his heart—Subaru." It charms me that the president of what sounds like a cement truck company would quietly cherish a beautiful name. In his heart. That's from the Subaru Global web page, btw, so you can believe it.

Subaru means "to govern" or "to gather together" and is the Japanese name for the star cluster we call the Pleiades, or the Seven Sisters. We can often see six or seven of them, and even up to fourteen. The stars are physically related, moving together across the sky. In astronomy terms, it's an open star cluster made of at least a thousand middle-aged hot B-type stars. Even sexier, the stars are blue. Hot blue stars.

It must have been the Greek myth of them that struck me as relatable the summer I was fifteen. Daughters of Atlas and the sea nymph Pleione, the seven sisters were transformed into stars after their father was forced to carry the heavens on his shoulders. Either they committed suicide out of grief, and Zeus turned them into stars, or Zeus turned them into doves, and then stars, to keep their father company. I remember lying on a cold green lawn at night, in Jamestown, Rhode Island, where my father had rented part of a house for the month of August. My sister and I were keeping him company, along with some ridiculously sexy women. I was well into the romance of suicidal thinking, along with the marijuana-induced, mind-boggling kinds of questions about one's place in the universe. What if our whole world is the size of a dandelion seed in someone else's universe?

The summer after Cade was diagnosed, at age eighteen, we rented a vacation house in Jamestown, its climate better for MS than hot beaches to the south. The five of us, husband and our three children, gathered together. We had shifted. We were possibly huddling, against an invisible storm. I would talk to the familiar sky or the cold salt water of the harbor where we swam, or the tidal river where we kayaked—the way back will be easier, the rental guy said, but the wind switched direction and it wasn't. The more we learned, the less we knew.

At age fifteen, in Jamestown with my father, I lay on the cold lawn looking up at the stars, at the edge of a cold stony harbor, and years later I wrote these lines:

> *Clouds of stars flicker and shift;*
> *Subaru gestures towards the earth,*
> *Waving an ivory scarf, then pivots*
> *Into darkness. Or it is high-flying birds,*
> *Wrapped white in moonlight, clustering*
> *In the cold air below the Milky Way.*

Actually I wrote "seven sisters" instead of "Subaru" but I thought I'd try out Subaru. Your past never leaves you, that's what I know.

The Big Time-Out

When she was young and said they were pretty, I gave my daughter the needlepoint strawberries I made in the mental hospital. I didn't tell her the mental hospital part. Two strawberries on a blue square ground. I haven't made a needlepoint in the twenty years since; haven't done a paint-by-number since chicken pox. We weren't allowed to smoke on the ward, and I needed to occupy my hands. Reggie, my fellow suicidal teenager, made detailed pencil drawings. Others played ping-pong, and those most severely drugged shuffled up and down the carpeted hall or watched television with their mouths open. The year I quit smoking I learned to knit. Haven't knitted since.

Being in the mental hospital was my first experience of being a spy. I wanted to act outrageous and be sent to the lock-up ward and write an exposé. When I went for morning blood draws, I could see the patients' faces floating up against the rectangle of glass crisscrossed with wire. Behind that door was where Elise went after electroshock erased her name. We took turns holding her head in our laps, her curls spilling over our legs; we kept saying "Elise" but she wouldn't claim it and she wouldn't stop crying and finally they took her from us. I may have been mentally ill just to assume that I was unlike the others, that I could watch us all and write about it. But the observing part of me felt most real, everything else a disguise.

I checked into the mental hospital on Halloween. My mother and I walked into the ward with a suitcase, and all around us swooped witches and Frankenstein monsters and rubber Nixon masks. Pointed hats, trailing sleeves like banners, orange face paint with a black spider web drawn over. I liked the whole scene. My new roommate Gina, an overweight Italian woman, sat in a flowered housecoat on her bed, muttering. At high school, I had just said goodbye to my handsome boyfriend Philip, who was luminously sweaty from shooting hoops in the gym after lunch. My motel room with Gina scared me, but it suited me more. The hospital appeared strange, a whole separate self-contained reality (like the Biosphere experiment, I think now), buzzing away up the road from where I lived. Carpeted and curtained, the room looked reasonably friendly, and undemanding. I don't know if my mother put my socks away before leaving, as she would a year later at college. After a while I sat on my bed and Gina turned to me and smiled. We each had our own twin bed.

At home in my twin bed, I would wake and call my friend Kate at 6:30 a.m. on school days so we could have our first cigarette and decide what to wear. Then I let the dog out and packed lunches and yelled at my younger sister to remember her homework, her library books. Our mother left early, commuting to North Jersey. Our father lived four blocks away. My sister and I liked to make spaghetti for breakfast, we watched the four o'clock movie after school and ate ice cream sundaes, we rode our bikes to buy the groceries and pedaled home. At school the classrooms were oases of order, but in between, the lockers crashed and the guys grabbed you and someone was getting stoned behind the theater. I could have been like Juliet B. who took ballet and stayed aloof. But I couldn't stop myself from answering questions. Why not hitch a ride home with the laundry delivery truck?

Nowadays we give our children time-outs, sitting them in a blank corner to think for a moment. It's not a punishment, the discipline books say, just an occasion to pause and change direction. I sit my daughter in the blank corner and she doesn't like it, but we're different. As a child, I always enjoyed being sent to my room.

I didn't feel lonely except when I fainted after blood draws and woke on the hall carpet near the lab with patients stepping over me on their way to breakfast. Then I was just one of them, another girl lying facedown. On my ward I got noticed for being young and not too messed up. The forty-somethings in for drug and alcohol rehab nicknamed me "Ivory Girl," which pleased me when they called it out. Other teenagers seemed hopeless: schizophrenic Steve, heavily sedated, dragging along in his black Led Zeppelin T-shirt. Of course I didn't see him as hopeless then. My first impression: *There's a really nice guy here named Steve—at least there's one person I can relate to—who says he's into rock'n'roll, which is cool.* Even half comatose, his blue eyes beamed a weird anarchic glimmer. "Hey man," he would say, raising one hand in limp greeting.

My friend Reggie and I had yard privileges. In the late fall, the lounge chairs appeared forlorn, grouped around a dry cement birdbath. We would smoke and walk the edge of a stubbled cornfield and I would stare down the road toward my other life. The Skillman School for Boys, a juvenile detention facility, lay nearby. I had volunteered there the previous year—me, a curer of waywardness! The next school along that road was Stuart, a Catholic girls' school which I had begged to attend in the eighth grade, attracted to the uniforms and prayers. But I was sent to Princeton Day School, the next institution past Stuart. PDS, for cool preppy jocks like Lily D., who could kick a soccer ball or throw on a pink strapless cotillion dress with equal aggressive confidence. I preferred the sideways cackle of Reggie, who had driven one after another of his father's farming vehicles into walls until he was sent here.

I felt at home with the sadness of the midlife-failure patients. Maybe their sadness felt familiar, the particular sadness of having to drop, after long struggle, all appearance of success. By the time I knew my mother's mother, she hardly moved from her chair in the living room. We had to hug her when we arrived, feeling her rib cage through the silky bathrobe. She watched television and smoked and ate candy and drank. Her hair fell out and she wore a wig, which she never brushed, flat blondish curls. And my father's mother, once grand and matriarchal, dwindled to an alcoholic widow during my childhood. She charred the Thanksgiving turkey one year. We ate it without comment. Then there were two uncles, my father's brother Bill who had been unemployed for years, and my mother's brother Bruce who had never had a job. The unemployed one, a Harvard MBA, still wore a silk square in his blazer pocket, but the act was wearing thin. The other one, always on the verge of a megadeal, supposedly in music but actually in drugs, only showed up sporadically, when he could bring an armload of gifts. My parents had gone to graduate school and they kept their houses well and adhered to the basic Christian belief system and the Democratic Party. We were safe, weren't we? Around us the relatives crumbled.

Dr. Sugarman gave me nothing. He asked clinical questions about the duration and frequency of the suicidal impulse; he nodded, wrote briefly in a notebook, twirled his chair around so I faced its high tweedy back. I wondered if he were German. The first suicidal impulse had occurred at age eleven. I snuck into the bathroom at night to shave my legs. When I picked up the razor, it glinted in the medicine cabinet mirror, and in the mirror I looked at the razor and it seemed to look at me. Did the razor beckon? I began to conceive of Dr. Sugarman as a German sugar man, enticing a column of children up a street. A cobblestoned street, and he walking backwards up it, offering lumps of colored crystal in his hand. Where were the children going? To the clinic. He told me I would never live a normal life without medication. The streets grew dark with soot, the fringes of the trees smoked in the November evening. The candy was a lithium salt. Dr. Sugarman was the father of a classmate. My classmate was normal.

My mother and I had walked into the clinic as if into church, hushed and abashed and dressed properly. We genuflected at the desk and signed forms for a twenty-one-day observation, a voluntary commitment. Voluntary, though strongly suggested by the psychiatrist I'd seen for fifty minutes after school one day. I had not been caught, as my friend B. was, with razor blades in my purse. But my arms were scored under the sleeves, and there had been the Tylenol overdose incident, my poor red-haired pediatrician standing over me with his blue eyes bewildered. We walked into the clinic as if onto a cruise ship, the director with her clipboard pointing out the beauty salon, the game room, the gym. Oh how nice, we murmured to each other.

My boyfriend's mother had spent time in this clinic. She was manic depressive, bipolar as it's now called, just as they said I was. Her husband had left her with seven children. How could she not have been crazy? Ordinarily Mrs. F. was a benevolent presence in the kitchen, her hair held back in a loose bun, cooking dinner amidst a sprawl of teenagers. Then she had rages, breaking half the plates. More than once the kids came home from school to find their rooms emptied into the upstairs hall, mattresses up-ended against the wall, books and clothes in heaps. "Your rooms were a mess," she said. "I couldn't stand it anymore. Clean this up." Insurance would pay for a few weeks in this private clinic and then Mrs. F. would be transferred to the state hospital where she lived, it seemed to her son, behind a chain link fence, surrounded by animals and ghosts.

My mother and I walked down the clinic hallway on Halloween as ghouls streamed past us and perhaps we seemed startled by a vampire or a Dorothy because the director said conspiratorially, "It's Halloween. We let them dress up." Having just walked in from high school, a little depressed, a minor troubled teenager thing, I wasn't one of *them*. I didn't hallucinate or scream in public. My pupils weren't dilated. I didn't drool. No dark circles under my eyes, no wild tangle of unwashed hair, no shuffling, slouching, mumbling, stuttering, not too fat or too thin, without facial tics, not trembling or sweating. Just swinging my hair, I used Breck shampoo, I could be a Breck Girl, turning my head to take in the ping-pong table, the silvery bank of pay phones, the patients' brown lounge, the line of diner stools at the snack bar. Then the director pushed through a door, explaining that patients on this ward could come and go. The locked ward held patients who needed to be confined. Yes, of course, we nodded in our tourists' way, but the possibilities dwindled for all of the tours a girl and her mother might be taking, for here, the director gestured, was my room.

The situation was fine because you just keep walking and put the suitcase down and nod at Gina, a mental case with a bad haircut who is huddled into herself over there, and see the beige curtains and the bathroom and your dresser and listen to the director say the bedroom door must be kept open for the safety of the patients and the lights go out at ten. Your mother asks about visiting hours and you unzip your bag, and there wasn't so much to dread after all. Now you are a patient. Back at school the students are passing notes in math class or giving oral reports in European history, but you are not in those rooms or on that schedule. The hospital is a manifestation of your inability to play a successful high school senior girl. This is a relief, because now you do not have to skip school and wander the empty house weeping. You can relax. The dining hall opens at five. In the morning there will be blood tests and an EEG. Maybe they will discover the source of your desire to jump off of the Empire State Building. *Isn't it good they have a high fence, Dad?* You had asked on the observation deck, in the innocence of age twelve or so, as if everyone might be tantalized into leaping. Arrested away from the view for a moment, he had turned to face you.

My father said he'd never wanted to kill himself. He had been depressed, sure, but never *that* depressed. My mother didn't say. Once she said that every time she had a headache she worried it might be a brain tumor, and I concluded she might not mind a heroic exit. (Actually she was afraid of leaving my sister and me motherless, but I didn't know that yet.) Suicide always got interpreted. The suicide had to become the proper, inevitable end of the story. I didn't care so much about controlling the narrative of my life then. Could one hang oneself from a doorknob? was the sort of question I fell asleep to then. And how much could one sleep? I could sleep after school for hours. In the hospital I couldn't sleep for hours in the afternoon; we had to choose activities. In the hospital I couldn't drink vodka and roam the dark town.

In the hospital I made a leather bracelet with a brass snap fastener. Reggie made a sculpture. I wrote a poem about a locked red box with bad feelings stuffed inside; the art therapist was very pleased. Reggie and I drank milkshakes in the snack bar, and we never touched each other. In the hospital no one touched me; people gossiped about patients sneaking sex in the bathrooms (the only doors we could shut) or being raped or semicoerced by male staffers, but not me. Goodbye to all that. The defiant gesture Reggie and I made was to sit on the hallway floor, our backs to the wall and our legs stretched out—instead of in chairs in the lounge. In the hospital Reggie made a fine drawing of a burning candle. We were mental hospital artists. Reggie sketched a cowboy in my notebook (he was from Montana). Another patient, Ron (older, alcoholic), wrote a poem in the notebook that began, "the world we live in says do or die, but I sometimes ask, why the hell try?" I copied out Anne Sexton poems and John Denver lyrics (how embarrassing teenage diaries are), and noted that a number of patients had broken arms from punching walls. I wrote: "I was so terrified of the EEG—they stick twenty electrodes all over your head and when you move or swallow the needles stick in sharper." I wrote: "I'm so pissed I can't go to that Grateful Dead concert." Looking back, I think I must have been out of my mind. (But am I out of my mind now? What will I think of *this* self in twenty years?)

About a month after my release, I swallowed all of my new anti-depressants at once, tiny red-hot pills. No one tried to medicate me after that. One night in the ER, and then weekly chats with a therapist who actually talked back. I thought I could still recover; I wasn't a chronic mental case. I've never gone back to the hospital, or taken medication. But there was no clean break out of prison, no shiny wave goodbye while riding a bicycle past the bare fields. I don't know for how many hours I've sat in a stupor of sadness, as if weighted by stones. How many hours in how many chairs. In the years before I had children, I might imagine overdosing in a motel, or escaping—taking a bus to Kansas, working as a diner waitress, renting a room, living quietly under a new name (always Barbara, I imagined). I willed myself to stay in the chair. Children complicated the fantasy because I couldn't leave them. The feelings would come, they always came, regardless of circumstance, in a sinister wave. This is why we speak of evil, of possession, because of the sensation of being occupied. The blade would beckon then, and the scratchy household twine, and the winking capsules in amber canisters.

One night, twenty years after the hospital, I am pacing in a tight square on the kitchen floor, arms crossed, crying. I must keep walking in a continuous motion until I can calm down. Then one morning I have the jitters, and don't want to drive the car or leave the house. One day I will be waving from my front door, I'll be the woman who never goes out. God, you are such a *mental patient*, I think. Just stop it. You want to sit in a lounge doing needlepoint while your kids go to school with their hair unbrushed? You can sit in a chair pulling the needle through hole after hole in a neat row, chatting with the others (hoping none of them will call you after release, like Ron from Florida did, asking for a date) about their divorces or the best brand of nail polish. Maybe Gina could be my roommate again. She started and ended every discussion with, "Honest to God, Kathy, you know what I mean?" She'd lost her memory. I could be there with her, existing in a limbo between life and death, the big time-out, but eventually I would have to choose again. My daughter doesn't want some sentimental souvenir of *Mom's visit to the psych ward*. My daughter doesn't want to feel like I do, ever, and what can I do? My mother loved me well, and yet—

When I was small, we crossed the English Channel on the ferry, and my parents said the best way not to get seasick was to stand on the deck. So my father took me up, and we stood with the other passengers, who were able to, in the cold spray as we plowed through clouds. I felt well, and very proud. Time passed, and then we stepped off the boat on the other side, into sunlit France.

One of the nurses rang a gold bell. The ward lined up, twenty-four of us in a straggled line down the hall. When we reached the head of the line, the nurse double-checked the name and placed two four-ounce paper bathroom cups on the counter. One held water, the other the pills. I remember looking down into the cup every time—pills are so pretty—but not the gray and yellow capsules. The nurses turned their faces to us as we swallowed, to make sure. I can't remember what the nurses looked like, only the whiteness of their skin under fluorescence. I remember the back of the doctor's chair, the dead grass, the cement sidewalk between the doctors' building and the ward building, the brown carpet of the halls, the plastic trays sliding along the metal rails in the dining hall, Reggie's pointy black cowboy boots, and the cashier ringing us up in the snack bar. How lucky we were to have money. One day I walked out into the neutral space that was the parking lot and crossed back over into my high school life.

Not everyone crosses back. Around me the relatives dissolved like sugar cubes, grandmothers shrinking, aunts and uncles divorced and disappearing. As a kid, I played with a set of brass scales my parents had bought on Portobello Road in London; I stacked brass weights on the brass plate and then filled the brass saucer with shells and stones until the scales balanced. Above the scales loomed an enormous yellow daisy in a red field, a wall hanging woven of coarse dyed wool that my Uncle Bill had brought back from Peru. Uncle Bill and Auntie Lynn had lived in Peru before moving to Connecticut, where Uncle Bill spent weekends restoring an old Austin-Healey convertible in the garage.

The word *before* infuses all thought of my aunt and uncle, *before* like a protective theater curtain I want to hang around their pretty house in Connecticut surrounded by woods. Before their divorce, before Auntie Lynn married a Mormon and gained a hundred pounds and had nine more children after our cousins Ian and Allison. Before Uncle Bill became an overtly raging alcoholic, before he was fired from what would be his last job, before all of this, Uncle Bill and Auntie Lynn had lived in Peru. They moved to Connecticut and had two children. (The very word *Connecticut* sounded safe to me, with its hidden silent "c"; when John Cougar Mellencamp sings "the cool green lawns of Connecticut," it summons up that feeling of sanctuary.) Uncle Bill commuted to work in New York City. Auntie Lynn gave me her childhood copy of *The Lion, the Witch and the Wardrobe*. Auntie Lynn had been a flight attendant. She wore her brown hair parted on the side and flipped up at the ends, like Mary Tyler Moore. Later she would cut it all off short, losing any pretense to prettiness, and she would wear a tank top and wave her flabby white arms about while we all stood on a hot concrete driveway in California and she explained her new life. A red-haired baby cried for her from its playpen inside. The new husband arrived, debarking smartly from his Ford Bronco with a gun rack on top. He debarked in jungle camouflage clothing with three teenaged boys. He and the boys had buzz cuts. What sort of life did our cousins have now, my sister and I wondered.

If only we could all go back through the wardrobe to the shelter of Connecticut, where I sat with Auntie Lynn in the wingback chair, staring at the green woods while she read aloud to me. Uncle Bill would always tinker with his silver convertible in the detached garage, and a few hours' drive away in Pennsylvania, the daisy they brought back from their newlywed life in Lima would always hang over the wooden dresser with the brass scales on top in the family room. Next to the scales, the small pottery owl would always look quizzically with its black-and-tan decorative eyes as my sister and I danced to the Beatles, barefoot, in bell bottoms, our long hair swinging.

Swinging

The Kindle is a great device because no one can tell whether you are reading *Marriage Confidential*, especially the chapter about swingers, or Alice Munro's latest collection. Apparently swinging is a secret to long marriage, and I find this hard to believe. So I did a little web search because the book said anyone could find a swingers club in their area, and amazingly enough to me, there was an establishment called The Cottage for swinging, in my rural town.

To be fair, the town also has a college, a seminary, and Civil War battlefields, so it is more than simply rural. "A social club like no other," is The Cottage's motto. My husband and I once went to a social club, a supper club in Iowa. We were served salads consisting of an entire head of iceberg lettuce cleavered into wedges. The Cottage is not like that supper club. Spouses supposedly go there together, mingle in a "party room" and then pick up extramarital partners and, well, you know. Call me dumb, but this defies belief. Yet you can take a virtual tour of The Cottage, with a bar and DJ, a hot tub room, and sweet little bedrooms with quilted coverlets and shams. One of the homey bedrooms has handcuffs hanging from the bedpost. A swingers website includes many photos of womens' butts in bikini underwear pitched up toward the camera, along with photos of middle-aged couples wearing bulky sweaters against the mottled blue background of a school photo. Seems like everyone goes to these clubs, barflies and bureaucrats alike. Is swinging what

America is doing while the chattering classes read aloud to each other from *The New York Times* and clip recipes for chicken posole? Or am I the only one doing that? Did husband leave the room in a distracted manner? Maybe everyone else is hanging out without me? I think I'll scrub the microwave tray now.

I live in a small town. Who goes to The Cottage? Does its culture include a confidentiality agreement like AA or Las Vegas or doctor-patient? I would love to go there to verify the actuality of the swingers phenomenon. Undercover work has appealed to me since reading Upton Sinclair's *The Jungle* in eighth grade. I envied Barbara Ehrenreich her undercover work in *Nickel and Dimed*, and thought that maybe in my older age I'd undertake a project like that, being a waitress or maid to see what it's like. Oh, wait, I've already been those people! Being a maid was much more fun because I'm voyeuristic. Also I dislike being shrieked at in a steaming hot kitchen, or frantically scooping ice cream for hot fudge sundaes, or making fifty anchovy-laden salads on a Saturday morning. Customers are never amusing, my smile notwithstanding. My smile was part of the outfit, along with a bowtie and suspenders. (Businessmen, please note: it is not ever charming to snap the waitress's suspenders.) Being a maid was a less stressful occupation, and I got to see peoples' stuff, their silverware choices and jewelry boxes and pajamas. Well, I would go undercover again—I felt that I adopted a persona that was not-me at those jobs, and at one waitress job, my boss misread my name and everyone called me "Kathreen," and Kathreen felt like an alternative version of me. Kathreen was cool with the restaurant owner cutting coke lines on the glass bar top; she didn't do coke but she was cool with its existence and with the owner feeling up Cherie the head waitress. Kathreen just sipped her gin and tonic and counted up her tips, smoothing out the bills. She talked to the 'Nam vet cook as if he was not out of his mind. I was cool with her.

I would go undercover again, but not at the cost of having sex with strangers. Or maybe they would be acquaintances. I'm dying to know if I know anyone who goes to The Cottage. Why? I'm a nosy, curious gossip, that's why. According to *Marriage Confidential*, an "Oreo marriage" is "traditional on the outside, untraditional on the inside." Could it be true? My fellow townspeople seem so proper, with their tasteful landscaping and tailored clothes, their unwillingness to say the least controversial thing. Tell me my neighbor is crawling fetchingly across an orgy room in all-white lingerie and I will laugh in relief. In *Reality Hunger*, David Shields writes, "I'm interested in knowing the secrets that connect human beings. At the very deepest level, all our secrets are the same." Do my fellow townspeople have this particular secret? Husband would have to down seventeen vodka-and-sodas (low-carb) even to contemplate such an adventure, and then he'd be no good at all, would he?

The Kindle is compact and lightweight. You can buy a book in thirty seconds and drop it in your purse. It is excellent for traveling, especially in non-English-speaking countries.

Wayward

It's hard to imagine, now, how it was that I took up with that boy in South Carolina, but facts are facts. William Buchanan Redmond was lawless and drawling, full of sideways glances and outrageous proposals. He went by "Cannon." One night on Hilton Head Island, where I was staying with a friend's family (thanks to private school I now had friends with houses on Nantucket, etcetera, though I lived in a modest house with my mother and sister that we were renovating to resell), he approached me at an outdoor concert. A man was playing a sing-a-long rendition of "Take Me Home, Country Roads" in the piazza down by the harbor, hired by the resort to entertain visitors while they strolled and ate ice cream. Cannon sat down next to me on a brick wall. I thought he was cute. I'd say something more intelligent, except my teenage diaries reveal a definite simplicity of thought: He was cute. He was cool. He was dealing drugs out of a purple van in the parking lot.

When he sat down next to me, he said, "Hey." I said, "Hey," back. Then we smoked cigarettes. I was smoking two packs of Newports a day, fat white cigarettes in a green box: menthol. Supposedly tiny particles of fiberglass were embedding themselves in my lungs with every inhale, but I didn't care.

At night Cannon liked to sneak onto other peoples' sailboats, and trespass on the famous golf course. He liked to drink liquor straight from the bottle, and smoke joints. He smoked joints during the day, too, in the bathrooms of fancy resort hotels. Then he'd sit by their swimming pools as if he were a guest. But he wasn't. He lived with his parents and a bunch of little siblings outside of the "Plantation" of Hilton Head, the Plantation being the corporately owned and moneyed part of the island where tourists stayed. The landscaping changed as soon as you left the gates to the Plantation, from a manicured lushness to scorched crabgrass. I was taken aback when I saw Cannon's house, the sagging porch and brown yard set directly on the highway. But I was deep into it by then. "Wanna do it," he'd say in the drawl, with a crooked smile. We speak of "giving the bride away." I was giving myself away.

One night when we were lying down together on a deserted beach, he told me about a murder. A woman had been killed a few towns away, raped and strangled, her body left in the bathtub. She wasn't killed on the Plantation, but in a coastal town I didn't know. Cannon knew where it was, he told me how to get to her house, a two-story white house he said, and she lived on the second floor. I pictured the single white porch light shining down on the wooden stairs to her apartment. "Her name was Sheila," he whispered. "You think I coulda done that murder?" I laughed. "I know stuff that wasn't in the papers," he said, low and sinister. "I wasn't with you that night." He clasped his hands around my throat. "You think I coulda done that murder?"

It was just possible.

Cannon's first visit to me at home in New Jersey fell through because he stole a car. His father called to tell me Cannon was grounded. When he finally arrived, he walked off the plane wearing mirrored sunglasses. He carried a small nylon bag, in which he had packed a few essentials: T-shirts, a Confederate flag, a lava lamp, and an axe. (Remembering these items, I can't help but ponder airport security in the 1970s.)

In the guest room, he draped the Confederate flag over the back of the sofabed. He plugged in the lamp and watched, satisfied, as the blue globs started ovulating up and down. He put the axe under his mattress. Made him feel safer, he said. Finished with settling in, he turned for the kitchen. I followed him. I wondered if he had ever traveled anywhere before. He asked my mother for eggs—raw. He broke three into a glass and drank them. My mother and I stared at him. He hadn't even stirred in the yolks. They had stacked up 1-2-3 in the glass, like the lava lamp.

This particular embodiment of the South didn't play well up North. I took Cannon to a party and left him with a bunch of guys drinking beer in the yard. One of them came and found me. "I'm really sorry," he said, "but we had to beat up your boyfriend." The next day Cannon thought he'd frighten me for fun, by putting panty hose over his head and threatening me with a wooden hairbrush. My mother happened to see him coming out of the bathroom in his getup. She gave him fifteen minutes to pack his things. "I'll come back for you baby," he assured me. "Someday you'll see a dude pull up to your house in a black BMW with tinted windows, and it'll be me. You'll hear a motor gunning in the driveway, you'll run to the window, and it'll be old Cannon. Come to take you away." My mother took him to the airport. His father sent him away to military school. I haven't heard a word since about William Buchanan Redmond, my love of the South.

I loved the South, with its Edenic overgrowth, its excesses and extremes. The landscape expressed my feelings of wildness at the time. At home I chose oblivion and wandering. My friend Howie once carried me on his shoulder up the whole quarter mile of driveway to my dad's apartment on a cattle farm. I was too drunk to walk. "Here she is, Mr. Rhett," he said cheerfully, dumping me on the couch. My dad laughed.

My dad was in a stage. He had a waterbed with brown satin sheets. My sister and I liked to lie on it and watch TV in his room. Periodically when the mattress became too gurgly, we were allowed to take off the sheets and remove air bubbles by coaxing them along toward the release valve with a yardstick. Then we'd remake the bed and watch more television. We ignored the stack of *Oui* magazines in the television cabinet. *Oui* was pornography for gentlemen; the title was French, so it must be in good taste. My dad had a girlfriend with dyed blond hair and bright blue eyes, who drove a sexy red Mazda sports car. My dad loved Mazdas. He had a friend who raced Mazdas, and took us to see him race at Watkins Glen, in the "600," in which cars roared around a track for hours. Even to my untrained eye, I thought my dad's girlfriend was too obvious—her bathing suit was a crocheted string bikini. She gave me hand-me-downs: a pair of thigh-high blue suede boots. Her hair would have looked better brown.

My dad drove a green Porsche convertible, a 911t. (The "t" stood for "Targa." I liked knowing this, being in the know, holding onto the secret words like stones.) My dad gave rides to my friends, driving eighty miles an hour. He came to weekend soccer games at my school and stood with me on the sidelines. "He is a hurtin' puppy today," he once observed about a boyfriend who was completely hungover and struggling to run the length of the field. He yelled, "Give it some legs!" My mom was away once and he came by the house unannounced to check on me. Looking over my shoulder, he saw a crowd in the kitchen, a beer bong on the counter. The stereo was blasting The Doobie Brothers and I was flushed, wearing dangly earrings and my favorite purple shirt. "Hey, Ace," he said mildly. "Looks like you've got it all under control. Call me if you need anything, will ya?"

I don't know how my sister put up with me. It was that night, I believe, that I cut the hair off all of her Barbie dolls.

My mom was in a stage, too. When I had arrived home from South Carolina, there was no one at home. My sister was at camp. I had wandered through the empty house. Everything looked organized—even the row of men's shoes lined up neatly at one side of my mother's bed. I paused at that. I poured a glass of lemonade and sat in the backyard to think about it. My mom pulled up in her pink BMW. I loved that car, the BMW 2002, in deep rose. She'd bought it used, of course, like all of our family cars. She buzzed back and forth from our little townhouse in Princeton to her new job as counsel to the governor in Trenton. Her public defender's job had become frightening when clients threatened her, and us. She visited them in the Trenton prison and the Vroom Building for the criminally insane, where she'd once gotten locked in by mistake. She felt safer in her new job, designing the legalization of casino gambling, among other things; working with the Mafia was safer than defending the violent poor. I heard the emergency brake cranked up, and then she hopped out of the car, in tennis whites. "Honey!" she exclaimed, coming over to hug me. "You're home early!"

"A few hours," I said grudgingly, watching a man get out of the car in tennis clothes. He looked young, with wavy brown hair and brown eyes. He was sort of pigeon-toed. Cute.

"This is Bruce," my mom said. He came over to shake my hand.

"Hi," I said. "Are you living here?"

They both looked embarrassed for a second, and then they didn't. He was a lawyer, too, younger than my mom. He was living with us. He bought a book about disco dancing and taught us the steps. It was the year after *Saturday Night Fever*. When my dad took me and my sister to France the next month, we saw *La Fievre de Samedi Soir* playing in theaters. The fever of Saturday night in America had struck all of us.

I was perfect, and I was trouble. I did my chores at home, and rode my bike to the drugstore, supermarket, and dry cleaners. I could steer with one hand and hold my mother's clean blouses and suits with the other, the plastic bagging streaming out behind like a banner. I cooked and cleaned, and painted the porch. I babysat in the neighborhood for money. A good student, I spent hours on the weekend writing essays for English class, memorizing chapters of history. I dressed neatly, and didn't break the rules. And I was a jerk, hanging out my bedroom window blowing cigarette smoke into the backyard, hiding bottles of vodka in the closet. I talked for hours on the telephone at night to my friends. Once my friend Camie and I both fell asleep while on the phone with each other, the receivers cradled on our pillows. We were both grounded for that one—there could have been an emergency and no one would have been able to call. I was always either grounded,, not grounded.

As a townie in Princeton, I practiced breaking into university parties. Their version of fraternities and sororities was eating clubs, housed in former mansions along Prospect Street. If my friends and I couldn't get past the front doorkeeper, we would climb in a side or basement window, a window always being open for air in the rooms where people jammed together dancing, shouting, and drinking beer out of plastic cups. So many sweating, shining faces. We sneaked into Princeton reunions, too, a standard townie civic duty. If we were lucky, we'd have extra badges from a genuine alum, and if not, we'd find byzantine routes through dormitories in which a window or door would let out into a tented area.

I was trained in subterfuge by my dad, the only member of his generation I knew of who faked his way into reunions. Probably my sister and I were good cover—who would try to bust into reunions with his kids? He preferred the front door method, sliding in with a crowd of entrants, or pretending he'd lost his badge, and he looked the part, in his usual polo shirt, khakis, and boat mocs. He actually owned a boat in those days, a Bristol twenty-nine-foot sailboat. ("A Bristol 29," I would say airily, and I knew, too, how to raise and fold the mainsail and jib.) We were seldom turned away at the gate, and a memorable triumph was a free roast beef dinner from the Class of 1955.

One night I wandered off, home from reunions by myself. We lived in town, I had a curfew, so there I went. On the way I got sidetracked by a new building on a street near campus. Funny I hadn't noticed it before, a white building with many windows, manufacturer's tape still on the glass. Could I see inside it? I pushed on the nearest door, and it opened. I glided along the shiny floor. When a staircase appeared, I climbed it to the top. A large classroom opened up, a laboratory outfitted with pristine work stations, Bunsen burners never used, countertops never spilled on. Plastic wrapping still covered faucets at sinks along the wall. I walked from station to station, imagining how the classroom would be in daylight, full of students and beakers and blue flames. I touched the plastic faucet wrappings. I was here first. Arriving at one end of the room, I looked out of a large window. The street seemed far down. It occurred to me that I was in an empty four-story building in the middle of the night. Hurrying downstairs, I felt shivers in my back.

Stupid to be out alone. Pushing open the door as quietly as I could, I peered around. The thought of Stanley the Bum came to me as I walked quickly away from the building, toward home. I had taken Stanley the Bum to court, in the brick courthouse at the end of Nassau Street, for harassment. My friends called him Stanley the Bum because he did appear to be a bum, poorly dressed and hanging around the streets. He'd been following me around for months, which I didn't want to believe when my friends pointed it out, but when I did errands in town he was often in the same store, staring at me, black eyes in a dumb soft face. He seemed slow and strange, his pants belted up too high. He often stood still staring, while people bustled around him. One day he stood behind me in the grocery store line with a basket of things, and when I'd finished paying he set down his basket and followed me out. He stood next to me while I unlocked my bike and put groceries in the basket, and then I rode away fast without looking back.

He found me on a summer morning in the park at the end of my block, where I was babysitting my usual group of toddlers. When I pushed one on a swing, he got on a swing. When I rocked a little boy on a hobbyhorse, he got on the next one and bobbed crazily back and forth. I ignored him. When we all got in the sandbox to play, he climbed in, too, sitting on the opposite edge with his shoes in the sand. Black lace-up shoes. He looked at me, he'd never stopped looking at me. "I've got something for you," he said.

"Get away from me," I said.

He held up a box. "It's a pearl ring."

"I don't want it." I smoothed the sand for a play highway. The kids shoveled and patted.

"It's a real pearl. I got it just for you."

Now I looked at him. "Where would you get a real pearl?"

He threw the box across the sand. "La Vake," the name of the good jeweler in town, was stamped on it in silver script. My friends and I coveted jewelry from La Vake, distinguishing ourselves from one another by favoring different silver bracelets, or St. Christopher's medals, which supposedly protected travelers, in either red, blue, aqua, or green. The La Vake box was at my feet in the sand. "I don't want it."

He looked at me harder. "Open it. I got it for you."

"Take it back," I said, "and get out of here."

At this Stanley lunged full-body across the sand, grabbed the little box, and came up on his knees. I was on my feet pulling one of the kids out of the sandbox when he did it—took a handful of sand and threw it in the children's faces. Right at their eyes. "Get out of here," I yelled, "you asshole!"

Stanley gave me a sideways smile, delicately plucked up the box, and strolled over to ride a hobbyhorse. There were other people in the park. "Someone call the police," I asked. My kids were crying. I sat them on the edge of the sandbox and wiped their faces, and started putting on their shoes. The police came and took Stanley away in handcuffs. He didn't resist, just shot me a taunting look over his shoulder.

I had to go to court that afternoon and describe the incident. My mom came home from work. I had a court-appointed lawyer. Stanley represented himself. This was the most frightening part, to find that Stanley had two personalities, for there he sat behind a table, utterly articulate and sharp. After I told my story, he questioned me, without a shade of the weird sidling lust he'd shown before.

"Did you, or did you not, use foul and scatological language in reference to me?" he asked, tapping a pen on the table.

I must have turned pink. I was under oath. Not sure what scatological meant, I knew the meaning of foul. The judge looked at me—he was a friend of my mother's. My mother looked at me from the front row of seats, and the collection of individuals there in the courtroom with matters on the afternoon docket—they looked at me, too.

"I did not," I said. Everyone except Stanley looked satisfied.

He gave me one dismissive flicking glance and went back to his paperwork.

Stanley the Bum was thereafter banished from the township of Princeton, and forbidden to have any contact with me. The judge was grateful, because though Stanley had been stalking young women in town for years, he had never touched anyone, and so they could accuse him only of being creepy. Once he had thrown sand in the children's faces, he became criminal. Banishable, from the castle of Princeton.

Stanley knew where I lived, my lawyer had said. As counsel, he had my full name and address. So when I realized, in the brand-new university science building, that I was stupidly alone at 1:00 a.m., I shivered with the thought of Stanley, Stanley who seemed slow but threw himself across the sandbox so fast, who wanted me to have a ring, who knew I lied in court. I shivered with the thought, too, of the recent "bicycle rapist," as yet uncaught, who pushed girls off their bicycles to attack them. Funny how safe I always felt on my bike, as if I could fly right past trouble. I practically ran the ten blocks home, staying in the street where the light was.

I made it home, I always did, and I didn't stop straying. In those days the university library, the formidable Firestone Library with vast underground floors, was open to town residents. I would go to do homework, and wander through open stacks on the dimly lit lower floors. In the most remote areas, you pushed a button for a light, which would stay on briefly. I would walk through the light, and feel it extinguish behind me. I would see no one down there as I passed thousands of books. Abandoned card catalogs lined an obscure corridor. Vanilla cards still filled the drawers. Study carrels were tucked into corners, where oversized books leaned and crumbled. Then I'd come upon a lone reader at a table, in an isolated bubble of light. I would pass quietly, both of us silent as fish. In the surrounding gloom I would pull out a book and pause to leaf through, then put it back. One day I would be a university student, but not yet. I felt invisible, anonymous, an unseen wanderer.

One night in a town parking lot I tried to break into cars. Just the unlocked ones. I wanted to sit inside and pretend to drive them. My boyfriend at the time, a nice wholesome one named Billy, was beside himself, his blue eyes earnest and panicked. What was I doing? We'd been drinking, of course. All my friends did. We would drink so much of certain liquors that we could never drink them again in our lives: sloe gin, Southern Comfort. We drank vodka and beer and a jug wine called "Mountain Chablis." We would drink on the Revolutionary War battlefield, or in someone's house whose parents were on a cruise, or in a car as we glided up and down the hills of rural roads. That night I tried to break into cars, and occasionally I hitchhiked home from school; I was a tramp and yet an innocent, and so many strange men on the street saw this in me that I had a fake name at the ready. Barbara was my fake name, I don't know why, except it sounded superficial and elusive, like a wave.

It was possible to leave your life and not come back. Stanley the Bum must have once been a different person—a lawyer, maybe. Once, he might have been a thoughtful dark-haired child who collected comic books. The university students had all been someone else before they sat in their islands of light, studying, transforming themselves. "When I get my own apartment, that's what I'll have," I would say importantly to my mother, pointing at a magazine picture or dishes in a department store display, imagining a future self.

I could slip away and not get caught.

"Gone south," people will say about a failed business. When women tell their stories of lost virginity, I still don't tell mine, all these years later. It's to my shame (now softening into amusement as the years pass) that Cannon's seduction line, as we lay on the swaying bunk of a stranger's sailboat cabin in the Harbortown harbor, was, "Wanna fuck?" The Anglo-Saxon word is of the body, physical and direct. I consented, half unconscious. Boys wanted my body. Their lust wasn't personal. And what was my body to me? I was tired of fighting over it. My mind was separate—my mind that says: "fuck" came into the language in its current spelling circa 1495, the time of

Columbus. In the sailboat, peripheral light sliding up and down the small windows as the boat rocked, I was sixteen. The South Carolina coast held the bright green and silica glitter of early summer. Way back in my family history, it is rumored, one of the ancestors owned Hilton Head Island. Now, a couple of centuries later, in my personal history, the island owned me.

Little Farm

The styrofoam incubator holds twenty-four hatchlings. Two plastic windows in the lid allow a view of the eggs. An electrical cord for a heating unit is threaded through the lid. A red indicator lights up when the heater is active. Inside, the temperature is a constant one hundred degrees and the air is humid, thanks to a dish of water under a wire screen that holds the eggs. The eggs lie still. Third graders have marked the eggs X on one side and O on the other, with pencil. The eggs must be turned three times a day, from X to O and back again. The turns are recorded on a log sheet, along with the temperature and time. The hatch cycle is eighteen days.

I like egg-sitting the hatchlings. On two Fridays we have picked up the incubator from school, and on Mondays we return it. To transport the hatchlings, we load them into egg cartons, and place the cartons inside the incubator for the drive. At home we un-carton them. It feels weird to put the hatchlings into grocery store cartons, as if they were ordinary food. I have a pang of worry that they could be mistaken for unfertilized eggs, egg-napped for omelettes or brownie batter.

The hatchlings will become adoptable, and I wish we could have chickens, but our six animals already strain the household laziness. In the morning and evening there are rounds of chores, the dispensing of kibble and parsley, the filling of water bowls. Litter must be cleaned, bedding changed, dogs walked. Our dogs are maniacal barkers, ferociously defending our fenced yard from every motorcyclist and toddler who has the bad judgment to pass by, and so in the mornings I take them out in the yard on their leashes so they won't wake our nice neighbors. At 6:40 a.m., standing in the wet grass in rubber boots and a bathrobe, I feel a sharp sense of absurdity. It may be even more absurd that I've paid forty-two dollars for a French plug-in pheromone diffuser that may or may not stop two of our cats from peeing in each other's perceived territory. The disputed strip of land is our upstairs hall, which happens to be carpeted. Pets are cheaper and better than psychiatric treatment, is our parenting theory, but how many pets does it take to soothe the anxieties of our little brooding brood? It has come to this: two pets per child. Oldest child doesn't even live at home anymore. Yet her guinea pig hangs on, nibbling and clucking. Her nasty little dog lives to snarl another day.

Publishing has gone to the dogs, my husband says. Indeed it has. Jon Katz has a new book on dealing with the tragedy of losing a pet: *Going Home: Finding Peace When Pets Die*. Susan Orlean has devoted her fantastic talents to the subject of Rin Tin Tin. In the past thirty days, there have been 810 books released on the subject of dogs, according to Amazon.com. How to understand dogs, dogs' purpose in life, how a dog saved my mind/child/marriage/country. Last year when Jacob adopted his dog Hobbes, I thought of writing a little piece titled, "Hobbes: The Dog That Blew the Roof Off Our House," because I thought one more pet would blow the whole domestic operation sky-high—it was just too much. (Turns out I could have written that about his gas-producing propensities, but then thank god we realized we had to stop tossing him cheese cubes.) But why add to this ridiculously bloated market niche? If you search "Jon Katz Dogs" on Amazon, there are forty-five results. The man is a force not to be reckoned with. The point is, dogs have become so glorified that I dare not say they occupy a lower rung on the household ladder than people. No, they are probably spiritually wiser, more in tune, less corrupted. All their bad habits and lack of verbal ability are my fault.

I love the illusion of running a little farm. When we had a rabbit, I enjoyed crunching through the backyard snow out to her hutch to give her fresh water and carrots. I felt like a Minnesota farmer, bundling up in the morning dark, carrying armfuls of hay. However, my rabbit-tending chore took only ten minutes, and that is the beauty of illusion over reality: it isn't hard to sustain an illusion.

To what degree has embryology infiltrated the national third grade curriculum? How many classrooms are turning eggs three times a day? Who manufactures these clever styrofoam incubators? If only Susan Orlean would write about this! She has gone to the dogs, so I shall make a measly effort.

The incubator is a Hova-Bator model 1602N, available from Amazon.com for $45.99, via Incubator Warehouse. It was invented by the G.Q.F. Manufacturing Company in the mid-1960s, and by the 1970s they sold incubators with automatic turning cabinets, but we're doing it by hand here. G.Q.F. stands for Georgia Quail Farms, of Savannah, Georgia, apparently a force in the industrialization of egg hatching. Michael Pollan would wring his hands over this! We are perpetuating industrial farming with this sweet-seeming third grade class project. Pollan does conclude repeatedly in *The Omnivore's Dilemma* that people have to eat, and not everyone has access to locavore comestibles. (The world's population will hit seven billion this Halloween.) Isn't it excellent that you can buy a Hova-Bator on Amazon?

Susan Gregory Thomas writes that if medieval peasants could figure out how to raise chickens, surely we should be able to, and I have to agree. Though I was nervous about egg-sitting at first (no drafts! no direct sunlight! wash your hands!), I think I am not harming the eggs. I'm sure they would be better off if a big fat hen were sitting on them, fluffing her feathers and clucking, so youngest child and I do chat with them. He swears they are kicking and pecking, and he can feel it because he is ultrasensitive to vibrations (spiders are, too).

Our embryology project is under the umbrella of 4-H, which accounts for the cloverleaf sticker on the incubator. The four Hs stand for head, heart, hands, and health. If you join one of the 90,000 4-H clubs for kids ages five through nineteen in the United States, you will join sixty-five million current members, and say a pledge:

I pledge my head to clearer thinking,
my heart to greater loyalty,
my hands to larger service
and my health to better living,
for my club, my community, my country, and my world.

Written in 1912, the pledge seems to me inoffensive and inclusive. I'll worship at the sign of the clover. 4-H is run by the U.S. Department of Agriculture, and in addition to traditional egg-hatching projects, there are sexy new projects like the challenge to design an egg-catcher:

> *With billions of eggs being produced every year, agricultural, environmental, and mechanical engineer farmers must work to develop a means to collect and transport them safely. In this activity, design a solution to catch a single egg, and then test the prototype of your design.*

Youngest child is working with Bubble Wrap, styrofoam and cardboard, plus bothering his big brother Jacob for engineering advice. At 1:30 p.m. on November 4, the egg-catchers will be dropped off of the school roof. Say "prototype" to an eight-year-old boy and he gets to work. Say "drop it off the roof" and he will jump up and down. Youngest child says this is not true. He says that no one used the word prototype, and that he will not be personally dropping anything off a roof, and he is not jumping up and down. That would be undignified.

And youngest child can be quite dignified. Last night he volunteered to go onstage at the sold-out magic show at our local Majestic Theater. The magician strolled up the aisle, and plucked my little chick from my lap, where he'd been perched for a better view. Benjamin did not flinch when asked to put his head in a guillotine. He had to sign a liability waiver, and watch a carrot get brutally bisected, and then he cheerily laid his head on the block.

The Travelers

Across the street from my childhood home, the Weingards seemed like an ordinary family, until the silver Airstream trailer showed up. They parked it on the paved basketball court under the trees in their side yard, near the chain link fence that imprisoned their neighbors' aging but vicious German shepherds. They were travelers, and as I came to understand, we were, too.

My sister and I ran past the gleaming trailer every morning as we cut through the Weingards' lawn and woods, emerging behind snippy Dana Gilbert's butter-colored house. All she had to do was walk calmly out her front door and stand there for the bus. We probably had fallen-down knee socks and twigs in our hair. The Weingards' bosky yard had cherry trees in back, the lawn sloping to a creek and then overgrown woods. Their house resembled the woods in tone, a dull dark red. But there gleamed the Airstream, habitation of desert dwellers, poor cousin to a rocket. They were going to drive it from Pennsylvania to South America.

My sister could draw a map of South America, had learned back in Montessori school—where she also learned how to tie her shoes at an early age and chop carrots. Our elementary school, in contrast, emphasized rules and routines, such as copying out word lists from the blackboard and definitions from the dictionary. I loved this sort of rote exercise, which bred a passion for office supplies. South America, whether one could draw it or not, was exotic in our neighborhood where many of the residents had names that almost meant something in English: Mickelwright, Spicer, Miller, Nailbone, Weed. It's true that a Jewish family lived two houses over; Michael Levine and I had pledged, at age five, while standing at the bus stop, to marry when we grew up.

And if we don't? I said.

If we don't we'll push each other down this hill. We both stared seriously down the hill.

Yeah, I said. Which was daring in itself: in our house, you had to pay a penny for saying *yeah* instead of *yes*.

Next door to us lived the Miyakodas, Mr. Miyakoda being a geophysicist imported from Tokyo by Princeton University. We understood his job to involve the study of world weather. Noriko, my sister's age, had a room full of plastic telephones and cooking sets and pinball games from Japan, with many more hidden away to be given as birthday presents to friends. The family stockpiled quite a few durable goods, eighty rolls of toilet paper in the linen closet, endless packets of dried seaweed, rice crackers, and noodles in a bunker-like room in the basement, and Noriko couldn't or wouldn't say why, so eventually we wondered about their experience in World War II. When he wasn't tracking immense systems thousands of feet above us in the sky, Mr. Miyakoda taught us jitterbug dancing and judo. Usually, though, he covered the dining room table with awkwardly large charts and stacks of related papers and Mrs. Miyakoda would gently push the whole mass towards him to create a perimeter where we could set placemats and eat. She made us spaghetti almost always, figuring that's what we ate, but the sauce was eccentrically hers, unlike the tomato sauce we heated up with browned hamburger meat; her sauce was a delicate, onion-laced salsa.

I suppose that, when considered closely, every family seemed exotic because it was different than mine. The Finstons, for example, our neighbors in back, lived in a one-story home with a door to separate the living part from the sleeping part, a house of cool smooth surfaces with central air conditioning, tile floors and marble tables, and sliding glass doors all around. When birds flew into the glass panels, we were allowed to put them in a shoebox on the back deck and care for them until they died or recovered their senses. Mr. Finston, stout and dark, ate steak every night for his Scarsdale Diet, while his wife and twin daughters ate hamburgers or spaghetti (we were devouring numerous cows in those days). He wore slippery maroon bathing trunks at home, with no shirt to cover his round hairy stomach, and glossy leather slippers. In the living room, he listened to '40s songs on the radio.

I'll pay any of you girls a quarter to guess the title, he'd say. Then he would laugh sarcastically; we didn't know any of those songs. He paid fifty cents for a foot rub with Vaseline, but my sister and I would not do it and could hardly watch while the twins did.

Mrs. Finston, though exactly the same height as her husband, at five feet nine and a half, seemed by contrast bony, agile, and tall. A blond Irish Catholic, she liked to smoke and dance, neither of which Mr. Finston enjoyed. After attending Trenton High, which sounded foreign and urban though Trenton was right across the Delaware River from our town, she had earned a degree in landscape architecture from Rhode Island School of Design, and she paid us to weed her brick terraces. We had first met her as she mulched a tiered vegetable garden that adjoined our backyard. The Finston twins were just four years old then, playing with sunbonnets on, my sister was two and I was five. Mrs. Finston grew pumpkins, strawberries, and tomatoes. She believed in fresh air, ice skating on the pond, and even skiing on the short slope in the backyard. She was often disgusted with me and my sister for playing inside with Barbies. Girls should be independent and healthy, not cloistered with little plastic sex objects. (When my mother and father split up, however, Mrs. Finston did not speak to my mother for a year.)

The Finston girls, Debbie and Betsy, were our best friends. For years we all slept over at our house on New Year's Eve with a babysitter while the Finstons held a party and we spied on the grownups from our windows as they drank champagne and ate a midnight supper of fried chicken, the leftovers of which we got the next day. Mr. Finston, a nonobservant Jew, groused his way through Christmas and then let loose on New Year's. After midnight, he and my dad might wander over drunkenly to play for us "I'm Looking

Over a Four Leaf Clover" on kazoos, arms around each other though they didn't get along ordinarily. The song meant that good luck was always there if you just looked hard enough. Our fathers' last Monopoly game had ended when one of them threw the board up in the air. At the time that didn't seem unusual, but now as an adult, I find it remarkable that two grown men even played Monopoly, much less fought over it.

Several disturbing things happened in our neighborhood, such as our parents and then the Finstons becoming divorced, but whereas the details of those events are largely forgotten, other details remain indelible. I dared Michael Levine to pee down a drainpipe in our garage and my father sent him home. The way the sunlight slanted into the garage and hit the urine stream mesmerized me so that I did not hear my father come in from the yard. Another day the pack of us girls came upon Gary Westwater burning a frog, its belly exposed like the inside of a lime, with a magnifying glass in the Mitchells' front yard. We did not permit Gary Westwater in our yards after that, though he would periodically raid the Finstons' in hopes of stealing a turtle from their outdoor pen.

The worst incident, though, was when the McDougal dogs killed a dalmatian at our bus stop. One morning a dalmatian we didn't know was hanging around when the McDougal dogs, two black standard poodles, came trotting along in tandem. While we did not know the McDougals, who lived several looping curves away from our stretch of suburban street, we recognized their dogs. They sniffed at the dalmatian and then instantly the dogs were fighting, two against one, and we were climbing to stand on the split rail fence, the younger ones backed up against an adjacent oak for balance. The dalmatian was actually bleeding. Some of us owned cats, and heard them snarling and screeching at night and found them with a torn ear or a bite in the morning, and some owned dogs and had seen them snap, but no one had seen a dog set upon and ripped apart. What could we do? Would the poodles turn on us? I don't know how we balanced on the fence, but we were up there in a clump when our school bus pulled up, with Loretta the driver at the wheel. She opened her door and we stood, paralyzed and staring. I hadn't seen her get out of the bus before. Suddenly she was with us, flapping her arms and shouting for us to get in, and we did. She shouted at the dogs but they wouldn't stop. Loretta wore cat's eye sunglasses and capri pants between the eras in which they were fashionable, but she was stylish to me, and she could move fast. She grabbed her whisk broom and started beating the poodles with it, thwacking hard on their bony faces, but they did not pause. When she got back in she pulled the door shut and sat down. The dalmatian was on the ground by then. They're going to kill that dog, she said, calling it in on her radio. After school there were only the least traces of blood color in the blacktop's striations, and only then maybe because we were looking so hard.

I did not conceive of Yardley as a bedroom community of Philadelphia but rather as a self-sufficient town in its own right. Our ballet classes in the American Legion building, the lino floor littered with red bingo chips, did not seem pathetic. We stuffed the bingo chips up our leotards while doing the Mexican Hat Dance. Though the houses at the far end of our neighborhood were large, and generous with Halloween candy, I did not feel myself to be poorer than the people who lived in them. The children of Bangladesh were poor, and some children in Trenton, a half mile away across the river, were disadvantaged. After the assassination of Martin Luther King, Jr. in April 1968, we could see orange sky from our front steps. "Trenton's burning," my father said. In a week of violence, more than two hundred downtown businesses were destroyed and the mayor imposed an emergency curfew. My parents founded Action Now, a program that brought in Trenton's community leaders to speak at local churches, and Trenton kids for summer day camp. In January 1969, the *Bucks County Courier Times* reported that Action Now would hold "a series of interracial workshops and dialog . . . to foster intellectual and emotional understanding between people of different races and to stimulate involvement in community projects." In that time and place, my father called Cadillac drivers Nixon-lovers, and Nixon was a crook. (The fact that my grandfather, a Democrat and former union organizer, drove a Cadillac did not apparently conflict with this.) Children who were bored were unimaginative. Scabs should not be picked. This rule was difficult for me, and may account for one of my most vivid childhood dreams being about a priceless and well-preserved scab belonging to Queen Elizabeth I. Gum should be sugar free. Pound dogs were the best kind. Hand-me-down clothes and garage sale furniture were good. A gravel driveway was good enough; paving would kill the big beech tree. That's the sort of context that existed for me at the time of growing up.

Pappy Sams, Mrs. Finston's father, had built our house, which my parents bought for $37,500 in 1967. My father had just finished his philosophy dissertation on the newly founded British universities of the 1960s, which work had taken us all to London for a year, and then he was hired by the Educational Testing Service. We'd bought a Volkswagen squareback in Europe and traveled home on the *S.S. France*, from which my two souvenirs were a French sailor doll and a Batmobile. I brought an English accent, too, and could be heard saying things like, "Oh, mummy, what a lovely garden," about the blacktop playground. The day we arrived in the harbor of New York, all of our clothes and the year's worth of photographs, were stolen. (Luckily the thieves had left what appeared to be a worthless pile of paper: the only copy of my father's dissertation.) With no record of our travels, and new pajamas from Kmart, we had returned to America. My parents bought their first (and last) house together, my father had a new job, and we were making a life that would last five years or so and constitute what I think of as childhood.

When we visit my in-laws, my husband is returning to the house to which he was brought home from the hospital as an infant. His red high chair is still in the basement, his crib in the attic, brought out when our children needed them. His room is still his room, with a trundle bed, desk, and corner bookshelf. I cannot stop being surprised by this fact and wondering how it has affected him. Our home in Pennsylvania was the fourth place I'd lived by age five. After we left it, I would live in four more homes before leaving for college. The idea of my childhood home is made of recollection, assisted with certain objects such as the old French country-style wooden bed frames propped up in my mother's garage. Or certain floral bedspreads folded in her linen cabinet. I love the newness of moving to new places and setting up house—I'm a serial nester—though I am grateful for five years of being placed at a fixed point, so that every other place exists in comparison to 108 Glen Valley Road.

Glen Valley Road itself was pale gray with no center line or sidewalk. Our sheepdog Daphne used to stand in the middle of it and gaze up at the busier Yardley Road as if studying it. Once, a car gently bumped her in the rear end to induce her to move. A creek cut across our lawn and poured over a humble cement dam into a pond, too shallow for swimming and too small for skating, but good for catching frogs. Even our cats caught frogs, sitting on flat rocks and swiping with their paws. The very civilized elements of the yard—the stepped slate walkway bordered by pachysandra, and the beds of pink rhododendron—could be admired, but existed for guests, like certain sections of tourist towns, which the residents rarely visit. We preferred the strip between driveways where the creek ran clear over colored stones. Our sense of geography followed the creek, which originated beyond the Finstons' and flowed under a fence onto their property. Where it entered, the steep banks were packed with gray clay, which we molded into blobs and set to dry on a plank bridge. The creek opened into their pond, a large oval populated by bullfrogs, whose groans I fell asleep to in summer. Mrs. Finston paid us to weed the pond while floating around on a raft—the biggest we'd ever seen, made of concentric circles, sent by the twins' rich grandmother in New York. We'd clear off algae and watercress with rakes, and then, covered with slime, we'd slip off and swim, avoiding the feathery muck of the bottom. At the end of the pond, the creek flowed into a cement pipe under their driveway and poured out onto our property, a man-made waterfall. We liked the dangerous maneuver of lowering ourselves down onto the pipe from a high wall and sitting astraddle, above a realm of moss and skunk cabbage. Until one day Pappy saw a copperhead sunning itself on a rock there.

Pappy had built our house for Mrs. Finston, but she didn't, I guess, like the colonial style and managed to build a modern house in back, which became 108 and ½ Glen Valley Road. Mr. Finston's family had money; at the start of every season an enormous box from Bergdorf Goodman in New York would arrive, filled with one of everything in the twins' sizes. We would finger the dozen bathing suits, the shorts-and-tank-top sets in every color and stripes, too. Whatever the twins didn't like, my sister and I happily took. I don't remember meeting their grandmother, but I imagined a silver-haired matriarch in a purple Chanel suit, bustling through Bergdorf's and asking for one of everything in children's size eight as she hurried between departments. She had a chauffeur and lived in a penthouse. She seemed a different order of being from Mrs. Finston in her jeans and sneakers, Mr. Finston in his bathing trunks. He was a Trenton-based columnist for the Newark *Star-Ledger*. He wore a battered trench coat to work, and baggy khakis, and my impression is of untucked shirts and deli sandwich wrappers trailing from pockets. He often yelled at us for making a mess or being noisy, and he yelled at Mrs. Finston about dinner being late. What did he want from life? He liked to sit in his chair, which no one else sat in. And he was a train buff. When Mrs. Finston broke her back in a car accident during a snowstorm, Mr. Finston prevailed upon my parents to take care of the twins so he wouldn't have to cancel a long-awaited cross-country train trip. I did not think it was strange at the time that Mr. Finston was away, perhaps because he did not seem to be a person who took care of anyone, even himself. If Mrs. Finston was in no condition to wait on him, he'd have to go elsewhere. He left while his wife was still in the hospital. We girls had a two-week sleepover, answering our dream of living together. Later, after all of our parents were divorced, our mothers considered buying a house together, and we wished hard that they would. I often wished that our family would try an adventure, such as living communally or sailing around the world, like the Weingards driving to South America.

For the weeks that the twins stayed with us, my mother had to ready four children for two different schools on winter mornings, and then care for Mrs. Finston. Once Mrs. Finston came home, we would visit after school. She had to lie flat on her back on the white couch. We watched her read with prism glasses, and borrowed them to throw rainbows on the white walls. I was sickened by the thought of Mrs. Finston in her white Pinto sliding across the white snow and smashing into a telephone pole.

Her father was not rich. Pappy Sams lived in a modest rowhouse on the main street of Pennington, a house I first saw on the day of his wake. We always visited him at his bungalow on the Delaware. I knew nothing of his wife, who had died of Parkinson's disease the year before we moved to Glen Valley Road. At his two-room river bungalow he made iced tea from powdered mix and well water, in a tin washtub on the kitchen floor, which we poured into glasses with a dipper. The tea tasted slightly of minerals and tin. The sight of the washtub on the floor always made me feel secure, as if the world wouldn't change too much. His living room walls were hung with back-and-white photographs of the Delaware River Boating Club, men in old-fashioned swimsuits. In the river, we wore sneakers because of the sharp rocks, and Mrs. Finston instructed us to swim upstream, and then float back down to the house. We weren't allowed to float too far downstream. The murky water tended to a shade of brown, but held a pleasing temperature in summer. I loved the wideness of the river, and the vista of forest on either side. Circa 1970 proved to be a good era for river swimming: the river was cleaner than in the old days, when industrial waste from the fabric mills had caused it to catch fire, and it was more solitary than it would be in the future, with the increase of inner tubers, kayakers, and party boaters. We swam in the quiet, scrambling out for a while whenever a black water snake floated past.

I still feel ashamed at certain acts, like winging a baseball bat at Debbie Finston because I'd struck out. As the oldest, I was the natural leader of the five of us, including Noriko. At Noriko's wedding, where we all squeezed into black floor-length lace gowns and consented to have our hair styled and our faces made up professionally (my husband didn't recognize me), Mr. Miyakoda commented affably, "You girls were always so mean to Noriko." That did not seem a fair comment, as I had flown across the country to stand there in a tight dress and hairspray, but it is true that Noriko and my sister were the youngest, and she had moved in last, and after she had told us her name meant seaweed we would not stop teasing her. She didn't speak English well until she was seven, and when we made up a play, Noriko usually had to be the mostly silent Asian Prince. She stood somberly off to the side wearing royal purple, her hair tied back in a low ponytail, a black moustache penciled on. Our parents lined up on the Finstons' couch, watching us politely as we sang Carpenters' songs or improvised a royal drama. They must have been stupefied—they've told us so. Often they needed a few drinks to survive it, and once during our medieval housekeeping play with the recurring song, "Maids, maids, maids, all we ever do is work," my father jumped up and became the humpbacked sister, who chased us all offstage. Mrs. Finston once remarked, "You always had to be the beautiful princess." She turned her nose up, imitating me.

We children wanted an audience, but I did not realize we were seen differently than we saw ourselves. Nor did I realize how little I knew of our parents. Our family room ceiling, wooden with exposed beams, was painted half red and half white. My mother liked the red, and my father liked the white. The ceiling now seems a laughingly obvious symbol of their division, but then it was just our family room, where the furnishings were eclectic anyway: the wall hanging from Peru, a British hunting scene, antique rocking chairs.

Our family thought of ourselves as travelers, who could roam the world and bring back souvenirs. Not that we were souvenir hounds, but that over the course of our travels we would naturally accrue a few objects, as one would no matter where one lived. Our winter hats just happened to be Scottish wool tams. Our traveler identity meant more than money. My sister and I were supposed to be equally at home in the Action Now summer camp and a restaurant in Switzerland. We wore hand-me-downs but appreciated pearls, letting our mother's cascade over our fingers when we unzipped her soft pink leather jewelry case. Neither of our parents came from money. They had qualities of education and style that seemed to transcend money or class. Or, as well-educated people have been known to wish, maybe education *is* class. My parents believed they could do things and they did them.

The Weingards left for South America. Debbie, Joanie, and Brent, who were sixteen, fourteen, and twelve, took a year's worth of textbooks and homework assignments along. This awed me, not having dreamed that one could do the homework and skip going to school. They drove through Mexico, where Joanie met Klaus, the German hitchhiker she would marry years later. He was twenty-one, and midway through a round-the-world journey. In Mexico, Klaus fell in love with Joanie, and I could see why. She had just played the swan in our ballet recital of *Swan Lake*, looking supple and ethereal while we stood trembling to the side in our flower tutus. When the Weingards parked for the night, they would hook on the awning, assemble the folding table, and talk by lantern light, just as they had demonstrated in the side yard. They drove all the way to the tip of Chile. When they returned, we threw a welcome home party and Debbie Weingard made us guacamole, which we had never seen before. The grownups loved it. On the washed-out mountain roads, Mr. Weingard said, he had thought the trailer might go over. Mr. Weingard resembled G.I. Joe as he described pushing the tilted Airstream back to an upright position. Surely he hadn't been fearful.

Pappy must have had arthritis or heart trouble—though not overweight, he took a long time to extricate himself from his car. After he parked in the Finstons' driveway, he would push the driver's side door open, swing his legs out, and sit for a while. He carried tobacco in a yellow plastic pouch, and would sit and fill his pipe while we gathered around him; he carried candy, too, old-fashioned Mary Janes in red-and-yellow wrappers, and caramel creams, laid out in rows under cellophane. The parked cars were pulled up against a hill, at the top of which was a hollow tree. While we ate candy, Pappy reported on the creature who lived in this tree, a gnome, except pronounced "ganomey" to make it different. The ganomey lived in this tree, Pappy said, and we ought to visit and bring him offerings. The creature would hide from us, but if we were quick we might see him. We liked the idea of the ganomey, and brought flower bunches and creek stones to the hollow tree. The tree became our ceremonial place, where we buried the dead birds, even one found at the bungalow. (One of our mothers said, "Are you kidding?" when we laid the dead bird in the car trunk.) Sumac and thorns grew over the hill, which we didn't climb except to visit the tree. I don't remember whether Pappy suffered an illness or died suddenly, only that all of us girls accompanied Mrs. Finston to his wake at the funeral parlor in Pennington. I had never been to a service for a dead person; when my grandfather died in Indiana, my little sister had just been born, and only my father went. In the greenish parlor someone said, "Don't look or that's how you'll remember him," but I did look and that is how I do remember him, his face large and doughy because it didn't move anymore, his hands folded on his chest. Afterwards we walked to his house. Mrs. Finston had said she'd grown up without money, and now I understood what that looked like: a small living room, low ceilinged, with a worn couch and dingy paint. The room seemed to pall around the great height and energy of Mrs. Finston. She surveyed the walls, shelved with curios, and selected a pink fluted-glass tea set for my sister. She must have given us each a souvenir. My sister kept the tea set nicely, in a glass-fronted cabinet in her room.

Forces unbeknownst to children churn around a household. Soon it was the year our mother went to law school, the year our father almost took a job in Chicago. I wonder what our lives would have been like if we'd gone. We stayed, though, and my parents must have been hopeful as they planned the summer of 1972: my father would be a Pennsylvania delegate at the Democratic Convention in Miami Beach, and then we would all travel to Europe.

We loved McGovern, and wore T-shirts that said so, with a blue line drawing of the candidate's face across our chests. Mr. Finston scoffed at us. My sister and I worked with our mother at party head-quarters, stuffing envelopes, and sometimes the twins and Noriko came along, too. Hot colors beamed into our living room from the convention hall in Miami. Our family—living in a house on a quar-ter acre, close to our neighbors, residents of a small town—had sent a representative out into the world. We watched hours of coverage, straining for the image of my father. I don't remember whether we saw him, only the intensity of scanning the crowd, with their funny hats and placards on sticks. Which pinkish face would be his?

The Weingards had left the neighborhood altogether, Mr. Weingard having been posted by IBM (I've Been Moved, the employees called it) to The Hague, Netherlands. We would stay with them for a while. Traveling that summer felt joyful—we were the sort of people who boarded overnight flights, took Dutch streetcars, and wandered through the public parks reading plaques. We ate french fries in newspaper cones at a cold harbor. We played on the beach at Scheveningen in sweatshirts and jeans. We played with Debbie Weingard, who had just lived with us for the year so she could finish high school in Pennsylvania. Now I try to fashion an atmosphere in retrospect: my mother commuting to Seton Hall in New Jersey after having been a housewife for ten years, my father charged with fixing breakfast and packing our lunches on the days she had early classes, and Debbie Weingard living downstairs in the study. Our house had only one full bathroom. I wonder if families take in extra people at times of impending trouble. My sister and I adored Debbie Weingard, who gave us piano lessons and would play pop songs for us after she had finished her own practicing. She went on to study at the Boston Conservatory. She played and sang, "[What's It All About,] Alfie," "Raindrops Keep Falling on My Head," "Do You Know the Way to San José?," and "Sitting on the Dock of the Bay." Listening to her sing, in our formal blue-and-white living room, the de facto playroom unless guests were over, made me feel lonely and happy and desirous—maybe of being grown up and able to go places of my own volition. It wasn't so long before that I had threatened to go down to the garage and saw myself in half if my mother wouldn't drive me to Ott's toy store to buy a doll.

The Weingards lived in a tall row house on a city street in The Hague, with their dining room in the front window, as was customary. Mrs. Weingard made us pancakes in the mornings, and then, before heading out for the day, we watched the Olympics. Between the 1972 Democratic Convention and the Munich Olympics, my sister and I had never watched so much television. We watched the shots of hooded terrorists with machine guns. The station seemed to show the same clip over and over, a terrorist with his gun ducking down behind a concrete staircase. Upstairs I found a copy of *Lord of the Flies*, and felt mature to be reading it at age ten, judging the characters to be realistic, as opposed to the usual adult view of children as harmlessly blissful. If I wasn't scared of the world then, I think it was because I believed in the power of individual heroines. I had spent much of fourth grade writing a "novel" about a girl named Anna escaping from the Nazis. Uncoincidentally, I had read *The Diary of a Young Girl* by Anne Frank. We visited her annex in Amsterdam, en route to Klaus-the-former-hitchhiker's family home in Germany. Klaus's father, Herr Hubel, with white hair stood in his formal living room and told my father that he had fought in the German army. A Nazi! I don't know what I said or did to make my father turn hurriedly.

"He wasn't a member of the Nazi Party," he said, "bending over to whisper."

"The what?"

"He was drafted into the German army—he didn't want to fight."

"Like Vietnam," I said.

"Yes."

"Oh."

Mr. Hubel stood patiently. He still remained frightening; if not evil himself, he reminded me of evil—he was a shadow of it.

Klaus's little sister Anna, aged nine, showed us the basement passageway to the family's grocery store next door. Anna plucked green grapes off the produce display, eating them as she marched us around the aisles. She led us back through the hidden door. Invisible to the street, the dim tunnel felt characteristic of a complicated, death-filled Europe. We flew home on the day the Olympics closed, from an airport filled with policemen armed with submachine guns. Before boarding the plane from Amsterdam to JFK, my father was strip-searched; terrorists might be at large.

One night that fall, my parents and my sister and I marched through the streets of an unfamiliar neighborhood carrying signs, parading with a contingent of party members toward a rally for McGovern. We marched through the darkness of Bristol, an industrial town outside of North Philadelphia. Arriving at the Bristol High School gym, to hear the candidate himself speak, I wondered at my uncle Spencer stepping off the Secret Service bus; he worked for the party in Washington. I wondered at the crowd, the filled rows of folding chairs in a gym on a school night. My father introduced "the next President of the United States, Senator George McGovern," as a thousand people cheered in the bright, disorienting light.

At home there was no sense of trouble, except that McGovern did not win the election and my parents fought at night. I loved my bed, a twin four-poster in vanilla, with a bedspread of cool purple and green flowers. The night table had room for books inside; there was *The Vicar of Wakefield*, the first book I'd bought for myself—at a rummage sale—with an old leather cover and tiny print. There was *Ship of Fools*, bound in ocher cloth, which I barely understood. The attic door was next to my bed. Spiders nested in almost every high corner. I named them, negotiating that I wouldn't call a parent to kill them if they stayed in their places. Underneath me, my parents fought in the kitchen. I couldn't, or didn't want to, make out the words, but could distinguish their voices from each other and hear the vibrating bass of my father, the pitch of frustration of my mother. I couldn't sleep. I'd start to hit the bed with my open hand. I'd yell, "Stop it, stop it." Once, while they were hosting a dinner party downstairs I'd thrown up in my bed, and no one could hear me calling. Children, no matter how nice the household, often feel alone.

When they told us, they each held one of us on their lap, and they sat on opposite sides of the room facing each other, one under the white half of the ceiling, one under the red. Since half of American marriages fail, many such moments of telling occur every day. During this minute, somebody somewhere is saying, Your father and I have decided. . . . The understanding that they were going to separate, my father move out of the house, washed over me as I stared at my sister in her white summer nightgown. In the weeks after, our father left for a business trip to Boston and didn't return. If my sister and I have little memory of his departure, it is because he left little by little, taking another box every time he picked us up for a weekend at his apartment on a cattle farm in New Jersey. It is only now, many years into a marriage, that I stand—childishly, unreasonably—accusing.

Recently I dreamed about Mr. Finston's death. In reality, he died of a heart attack in his fifties. As far as I knew, he was an only child, but in the dream a brother arrived at the funeral—a young, handsome incarnation of Mr. Finston. I'd been wondering all these years why Mrs. Finston would have married him—a grouchy, fat, stingy man—and here stood the answer. The curve of his lips appeared wry instead of contemptuous, his nose well-formed instead of rubbery. He looked interested in sex, and not just via *Playboy* magazine (we girls found his stash). He was rich, but rebellious; he wouldn't live in New York City, he'd make his way as a reporter in Trenton, covering local ribbon cuttings (he took us with him once, to the dedication of a riverside park) in New Jersey's perpetually depressed capital city. In the dream I stared at this man and felt that ephemeral wisdom: I knew the dream of marriage and the dream that led people to build all of the factories and brick warehouses that stand vacant on the banks of the Delaware.

We had to sell our house, and so finally the living room ceiling would be painted all white. Mrs. Finston must have finished her year of not speaking to my mother, because she was helping, along with a collection of friends, who stood arrayed on stepladders. My sister and I ran to the basement for drop cloths and rollers, stirred the paint, washed the brushes. At lunchtime we were to make tuna salad at the Finstons' and bring it back. We were mixing it in a metal bowl in the kitchen when we heard a voice, Mr. Finston's, calling, "Who's there?"

"Just us," I answered.

He swung into the kitchen. "I could use a sandwich."

"It's for the workers."

"The workers?" He grabbed for the bowl. I clutched it in my arms and squeezed past him out of the kitchen. My sister and I ran to the back part of the house, toward the twins in their rooms. "Your dad wants the tuna and it's for the workers and we don't have very much!" One of us locked the door to the sleeping part of the house. He pounded on it. He yelled, "Any food that is made in my house is my food. My food. Open that door."

We opened it.

"Now you get out of my house and don't come back."

My sister and I walked out with the bowl, crying. He'd always hated us, hadn't he, the little Protestants next door, skipping off to church on Sunday, coming home smug with a box of Dunkin' Donuts. Once, he had been kind. Years before, we had been building a fort with loose bricks and a wall came down on my foot. He carried me inside and filled a sink with ice water and held my foot in it. He sang to me about a rainbow as we watched the bruises develop.

Recalling banishment, mourning your parents' bad marriage—what point is there to casting back longingly to the idyll? Adolescence was going to come along and change everything anyway. The junior high held six hundred students in a grade. Kids drank liquor from flat, curved bottles in the lavatories and stared at you if you'd come to use the bathroom. The social studies teacher showed career orientation films about factory workers. With few friends, I consoled myself with the idea that the rude popular boys would grow up to work in gas stations. I hung out with Rosemary, who lived one bus stop away. We wore baby blue eyeshadow, same color as our gym uniforms. We'd sit in her backyard on top of the doghouse and smoke. Her grandfather was in the hospital.

"How is he?" We had stolen two of her father's skinny cigarillos, which sent up a bluish smoke.

"He won't stop farting. I mean, you can barely sit in the room."

"Oh my god. Doesn't he get embarrassed?" We were laughing. A person could fall off the doghouse this way.

"There's no sound."

"What?"

"He pretends he's not doing it. We call them 'silent but deadly.'"

After that we taped each other farting, then played it back in the middle of the night during sleepovers. (There was no video, computer, or even cable TV back then for amusement.) Often that year I skipped school, walking out the front door as if heading for the bus, then hiding behind the boxwood hedges until everyone else had left. The vaulted space under the hedge brought to mind the England of Beatrix Potter books, the animals nesting under sandbanks. Once the irrevocable decision to miss the bus had been made, I usually felt calm, sitting scrunched up against the cool stone of the house.

Not too much more time would pass before my sister and I would understand the context for our childhood, that our town was tacky, our parents unimportant. If we as a family assumed an air of worldliness, we were to be hit with the real thing when our parents (well-meaning and cash-strapped) sent us to private school in Princeton, New Jersey. Not the Princeton of outdoor violin concerts on the university campus, where Mr. Miyakoda would smile dreamily at the clouds of music while we observed him. We met the Princeton of country clubs, families with Learjets, kids who skated in Sun Valley, skiied in Aspen, and summered in France. Someday I, too, would visit France in the summers. On the first day of private school I wore a denim overall dress with a blue gingham button-down, white kneesocks, and construction boots. Perhaps I was representing the Pennsylvania suburbs that just recently had been farmland. This new school lay dappled under a canopy of old trees, a gentle entrance giving way inside to a jolt of color as I walked into a crowd of madras and silver braces. The eighth graders seemed shockingly young at first because of their children's clothes: Izod tennis shirts, and skirts and shorts patterned with bright flowers and frogs. No one wore platform shoes or skintight jeans or halter tops or fake fingernails. No one slouched outside smoking cigarettes. The girls wore hair bands and ponytails and braids. Their hair looked shiny and simple. In the bathroom they washed their hands. The students didn't customarily cheat, and when a boy snapped my bra strap, he was made to write a note of apology.

We had traveled to another realm, just as most people we had known were moving: the Weingards to Asia now, Mrs. Finston and the twins to rural Bucks County, Mr. Finston to an apartment in Trenton. Our brief convergence in Yardley, Pennsylvania, was a dot on the time line. I pictured the routes of families on the globe, drawn in the curving lines of airline routes, the Miyakodas' long line from

Tokyo, the Weingards' running north and south on the American continents, and then east to Europe and beyond.

If you telescoped back a hundred years, you'd find Mrs. Finston's family, the Sams, alongside the Rhetts in the same parish of Beaufort, South Carolina. But we had all moved since then. With our transient ways, does anyone truly belong where they grew up?

Watchless

One summer day I was sitting by a bucolic farm pond with three women friends, and we discovered that two of us wore watches and used alarm clocks religiously, while the other two absolutely did not. How do you get anywhere on time, I wondered. Work meetings, school pickups? "There are clocks everywhere," Kathleen the librarian said. "Not wearing a watch helps me to be more creative," Wendy the artist said. Kate and I took off our watches to swim in the pond, and I announced that I would not put mine back on. I would try going watchless. Wendy and Kathleen teased me: "How will you know when to come back in from swimming?" They offered to signal me from shore, standing up and spreading their arms to show four o'clock, five o'clock.

I check my watch all the time, I soon realized, just as I had realized how obsessively I checked the green numbers of the microwave clock after it broke and I kept glancing at the black square that used to show the time. As a working mother of three, I thought that I needed to know the exact hour and minute, but maybe there was another way of living. At the pond, Wendy had looked up through summer-green leaves at the sky and said, "I can tell it's before three by the light."

Home from the pond, I should figure out dinner, but instead I curl up on the couch, with my son beside me watching television, my husband nearby on his email, and I fall fast asleep. Is this what happens when you take your watch off, I wonder when I wake up. You just fall out of time. You sleep when you're tired, you eat when you're hungry. This is the sort of lesson I'm trying to learn in yoga, to figure out what I'm feeling when it's happening rather than much, much later. All I had to do was remove this timepiece from my body!

In the morning, I see Kate and Wendy at the Saturday farmer's market. Wendy stands behind her table displaying beautiful silver jewelry. Kate has just bought goat cheese. "I collapsed yesterday, too," Wendy assures me. "I told the boys I was going to go work out, but then I lay on the floor with the fan blowing on me for half an hour first." Kate had fallen asleep in a chair, snapping awake when her husband got home from work. "Not only had he been out in the heat all day," she says, "but he had been working in it!" Wendy admires my watchlessness. Kate has hers strapped back on, and says firmly, "I used the alarm clock to get up this morning, too." This morning, I have left myself plenty of time to buy tomato stakes and produce, and then pick up the dry cleaning. "Dry cleaning" was third on my errand list, and my husband looked at it and said, "What's this, daydreaming?" I tell this to Wendy and Kate and we discuss how much nicer life would be if "daydreaming" could be an item on our to-do list every day. Maybe going watchless is a first step.

Going watchless during the weekend is one thing, but how will it work during the week? As an academic I am technically off for the summer, but my husband and I keep a tight schedule of work hours to advance various projects and administrative duties. One of us works while the other holds down the house. On Monday at ten o'clock or so (I didn't check the time) I have coffee with a colleague, relaxing into a long conversation. While my morning could be more efficient, talking with a friend is real and valuable, surely. Instead of surreptitiously checking my watch, I am going with the flow and it feels good. Living in Spain recently, I had noted that my friends there had better manners than I, in that they never seemed distracted or harried even when they had a lot to do. They looked me in the eye when we talked and did not seem to be halfway on their way to the next thing. Maybe I could acquire their social grace. Standing up after coffee, though, I see a clock and note with alarm that it is noon. I have to be home in an hour! Back at my office, a student stops by to discuss his summer research project for which I am a mentor. We're sitting at a table, with no clock visible, and I feel myself becoming distracted by wondering what time it is. I wrap things up and luckily will not be late getting home.

The next day proves tricky, too, as I attend student research presentations, and though I have built in an extra half hour in case the presentations run long, I am still ten minutes late getting home. (This may not sound like much, but my husband and I are careful of each other's work time—I still find slips of paper from years past when the kids were younger and the childcare/work routine was harder to manage, slips of paper with typed schedules of our work time in forty-five-minute blocks.) During the presentations, though, without a watch to keep nervously checking, I had concentrated more fully than usual.

A week in to my experiment, I realize that I am taking unfamiliar roads for fun. On the way home from minature golf with my six-year-old, I hang a sharp right into a battlefield road instead of heading straight home. We take a winding road through woods, driving slowly behind tourists, and the leaf-light is soothing. We are not in a hurry. At home, the clock reads 6:20 when we arrive, and I am surprised at how late it is—we usually eat dinner at six. But since neither of us is hungry yet, what does it matter?

Driving home from yoga class one evening at sunset, I try driving the high seam across battlefield hills. Usually I drive a straight line down into town, needling determinedly through stop lights and stop-and-go traffic. The battlefield route can be maddeningly slow, with out-of-state drivers pausing at every monument, yet not pulling over so that I can pass them. But the drive is across fields that fall away into green expanses punctuated by creeks and ridgelines. Turning downhill toward my neighborhood, I hover for a moment, all-seeing above the college campus, above the white steeple of the campus chapel, the playing fields and brick buildings. On another evening, I try a back country road—my new friend Kathleen lives in a development out this way, and I've never been back here. Missing the turn for my route home, I look for a turnaround spot and come upon a bustling campground that I would never have known about, and cross two bright tumbling creeks.

Back on track for home, driving along a field scattered with fresh hay bales, I wonder if taking off my watch is a shedding of the last vestiges of restlessness. My husband and I were nomadic until we moved to this town, and though we have lived here for years, we have traveled for most of every summer, and we have lived in France and Spain for sabbaticals. This summer we are mostly at home, and I am growing tomatoes, peppers, and marigolds for the first time. Let us cultivate our garden, I say. It's as if I have treated my town like the person whose shoulder you are looking over as you talk to them at a cocktail party. I've been on the lookout for a better place, the souvenirs in my home acting as totems. This year I have come to love my town and the surrounding country, the apple trees frothing with white blossoms in spring, softening into green in summer, and becoming jeweled with red and gold apples in the fall. Maybe I am finally not in a hurry to be somewhere else.

Thinking I have made a great new discovery, I tell my younger sister about going watchless and how much better it is. "Oh," she says, "I haven't worn a watch for years."

Crown

My husband speaks Danish, and he used to sing a little Danish song to me that meant, "Life is not the worst that one has—in a moment, coffee is ready." *Livet er ikke det værste man har, og om lidt er kaffen klar.*

It rhymed in Danish. Its sounds were odd and comforting, like a herd of white Danish goats trotting over a rolling hillside with their brass bells clanking. The melody beseeched its listener: *C'mon you, c'mon.* Its last note settled, but not resolutely. The song left an opening for the listener to answer. And so I get up, swing my legs out of bed in the dark of 6:24 a.m., click on the gas burners for espresso and milk. I froth the milk. The frother whirs its crown of wire. Now the brain is waking up. We are not, as people tend to say, hardwired. It's a metaphor that people use as frequently and confidently as if it were not a metaphor at all, as if we were snaked through with metal threads. The frother is wired, not me. My head is full of little songs.

In gratitude

Without Cynthia Lamb, this would not be a book. I am grateful to her, and everyone else at Carnegie Mellon University Press, especially Connie Amoroso and Gerald Costanzo.

Thanks to my family, near and far, for their love, support, fact-checking, reading of drafts, and general cooperation with being referred to, named, described, and quoted.

I thank my children, Cade, Jacob, and Benjamin Leebron, for putting up with being portrayed in writing. Cade, a fellow nonfiction writer, offered editorial suggestions, for which I am grateful. Jacob is a rather private person, and I hope I haven't embarrassed him. Benjamin is too young to read this, but does enjoy being quoted.

Thanks to my mother, Teel Oliver, for her steady encouragement, wise suggestions, and excellent personal library, all of which have kept me company over the years.

Thanks to my father, Haskell Rhett, for his thoughtful editing, family research, and philosophical sense of humor about my work.

Thanks to my sister, Cecily Rhett, my writing partner in various projects, and aesthetic kindred spirit, as well as emotional North Star.

I am grateful to the Leebron family, the family-in-law I am so lucky to have. Several of these essays were written in memory of my dear sister-in-law Kathryn Leebron Smyth.

For writing encouragement and sustaining friendship, I thank Barbara Jones, Cinda Gibbon, Jane Satterfield, Ned Balbo, and Jessica Handler.

Literary magazine editors have been kind and discerningly critical of my work over the years, and I thank Laurence Goldstein, Joe Mackall, Dan Lehman, and especially Christina Thompson.

I thank Gettysburg College for its longstanding support, my colleagues there for their friendship and inspiring work; and my students, for their talent, energy, and questions. Thanks to the Pennsylvania Council on the Arts for a nonfiction fellowship, and to the Central Pennsylvania Consortium for a Mellon Fellowship.

For my first friends, Betsy Finston, Debbie Finston, and Noriko Miyakoda Hall, who figure in these pages, I could not be more grateful.

Last and most, I thank Fred Leebron, my beloved co-conspirator since 1985.